# I Have Come To Set The Earth On Fire[1]

### Tragic Events Can Actually Be Blessings

By: John Chomistek

---

[1] Luke 12:49

# I Have Come To Set The Earth On Fire

Text copyright © 2016 John Chomistek
All Rights Reserved

Unless otherwise noted, Scripture passages were taken from the New American Bible Revised Addition. Copyright © 2011 by Catholic Book Publishing Corp., N.J.

Cover design edited and formatted by: Shawn Neal

This book is dedicated to the following groups of angels that have been a source of grace an inspiration in my life.

First, to my loving family - Cathy, Emily, Steven, Elizabeth and Ryan - for their spiritual strength, inspiration and love; the reason this story has a happy ending, or should I say continues to have a happy ending.

This book was written for Cathy's sister Geri that all crosses end in God's loving hands.

Many thanks to Greg and Angela for their work to develop the base design look of this beautiful cover.

Lastly, all thanks, praise and glory to my "Ghost writer", the Holy Spirit for His divine inspiration to live and write the fire story.

## I Have Come To Set The Earth On Fire

## Table Of Contents

Why I Wrote This Book ............................................................... 3

Chapter 1: The Lead In To The Fire Story ............................................ 5

Part 1: The Best Thing That Ever Happened To Me That I Would Not Wish On My Worst Enemy ............................................... 12

Chapter 2: Life Prior To The Fire ..................................................... 13

Chapter 3: The Fire: 7-4-96 to 7-12-96 ............................................... 27

Pictures From The House After The Fire ............................................ 46

Chapter 4: The Reality Sets In - Getting Life Restarted Again .......... 52

Chapter 5: The Face Of Angels ....................................................... 66

Part 2: Takeaways From The Fire Experience ................................... 80

Chapter 6: Humility Hurts ............................................................. 82

Chapter 7: Why Do Bad Things Happen To Good People? .............. 86

Chapter 8: Power Of Prayer ........................................................... 96

Chapter 9: God Given Gifts vs. Own Earned Wealth ..................... 104

Chapter 10: We Take A Lot Of Things For Granted ....................... 113

Chapter 11: The Essence Of True Peace ......................................... 118

Chapter 12: Paid Back In Full ........................................................ 123

Chapter 13: Doing God's Will Breeds Disciples ............................. 128

Chapter 14: New Appreciation Of The Beatitudes ......................... 139

Chapter 15: Go Tell It On The Mountain! ..................................... 150

Chapter 16: God's Most Precious Gift – My Family ....................... 158

Part 3 Closing Thoughts ................................................................ 164

Chapter 17: Jesus Is Relentless. He Wants Us All With Him In Heaven. ................................................................................ 165

Chapter 18: Review Of Things Learned From The Fire Experience .......................................................................... 172

Chapter 19: Final Concluding Thoughts ........................................ 192

# I Have Come To Set The Earth On Fire

## Why I Wrote This Book

When one goes through a personal tragedy experience, unbeknownst to the person or his/her family, their tragedy experience has in fact touched substantially more people and lives than just their own. It is easy for the person enduring the tragedy to look inward and get depressed because a bad or even tragic thing or series of events has happened to them. That tragedy could be such as a fire or business situation where everything owned is lost; a death of a loved one, especially a sudden one due to an accident or crime; a loss of a job or one of a number of other things that puts one into a personal and/or family tragedy situation.

We do not, and in most cases, cannot see God's purpose. We cannot project years or even centuries in the future to see how one's situation factored into God's overall plan for humanity. But every individual and everyone's situations – good and bad – does factor into God's overall plan. Just as a music note cannot comprehend its own contribution to a Mozart symphony, one does not have the complex and infinite vision to see and witness how their event fits into and is part of God's overall plan for humanity. As a single note is performed in a grand concerto, we all play a distinct role in God's overall plan for the salvation of humankind. Each one of us matters. As each note is played, one of possibly thousands of notes struck during the symphony, Jesus inserts us individually to enter into His song, His story of salvation – yours as well as the world's.

You will see in this book how my and my family's tragedy experience touched many persons in my community – ones that we knew as well as ones that we did not know at all. I am sure that God made this situation available to touch many more people that I have never seen or will ever know existed. God works in many and strange ways. Sometimes he works through individuals such as you and me. Sometimes you have to just sit back and let God do his wonder through you.

I have given the "Fire" talk to several different audiences now, mainly through church or church retreat events. Every time I present this topic, for one, has been a deeply spiritual experience for me, but also, from the response from the audiences, sometimes even years later, my family's story of living tragedy through the grace of God still resonates and touches hearts. That is why I decided to put ink to paper and provide the "Fire" talk to a wider audience.

As written by St. Peter in his first epistle, *"Always be ready to give an explanation to anyone who asks you for a reason for your hope."*[2] This book not only chronicles the events and things learned from my family's fire story, it also gives my explanation and my reasons for hope. Through my writing of this story, it has reinforced and fortified my belief and feeling of the infinite love and glory that Jesus gives and has planned for each one of us. We are not only figurative sons and daughters of God, we ARE TRULY His sons and daughters. If we truly believe that statement of fact, all is possible, even little miracles that happen due to one's tragic event; through one's saying "Yes" to their calling from God to do His will. If we follow Jesus' teachings and commit our lives to doing God's will, we will reap our ultimate glorious reward with Jesus in Heaven for ever and ever.

I hope you enjoy and are touched by this story as well, as this is my first attempt at the literary art. Especially those of you readers that have or are in the throes of a traumatic life event, know that God is working with and through you. You are a part of God's plan even though you may never see how this all fits together into His plan. May God's peace be with you for ever and ever.

---

[2] 1 Peter 3:15

## Chapter 1: The Lead In To The Fire Story

Let me start this book with a short prayer:
*Lord send down your Spirit to the readers of this book and we will renew the face of the earth.*

If you picked up this book to read a story of great heroism and gallantry, of heroes running into a burning home to save the damsel in distress, I just want to tell you that maybe you should find another book. On the other hand, read on because this story has heroism, but in the spiritual kind. It has gallantry, but also in the spiritual kind. It goes much further than that. It travels deep into living tragedy through the graces of God; to be a good steward of His gifts given; to follow His calling to do His will no matter the price.

What would you do or feel if all that you had was taken from you in a flash – similar to a Biblical Old Testament "Job" moment. One minute you are comfortable, comfortable with all the trappings and goods that the typical American household has grown accustomed to and takes for granted - house, cars, furniture, clothes, TVs, electronic entertainment and computer devices, golf clubs, bikes, tools etc. – you know, the standard living possessions. Within a few hours, all is gone. All is stripped away leaving you bare against the world with just what you came down from God with. This is truly a life changing event and what do you do now? How does this event "change" you? How do you think and go about your daily life from that point on?

This book is really a love story. Not one with two coming together and falling madly in love with each other. No, this is a book about the love of God for me, the love of God for my family, and the love of God for the world. Soon to be St. Mother Teresa once said, *"I am a little pencil in the hand of a writing God, who is sending a love letter to the world."* This quote best sums up the chapters written in this book, God's love story written through my family and to the world.

In everyone's life there are moments of transformation or conversion experienced that one can point to, which explains how one got to the stage of life they currently possess. But rare are there such events in one's life so colossal or life defining that the episode serves to divide time, a time or date of demarcation, dividing one's and/or one's family history into that lived before and that after. World history had that event. The world has had many wonderful and also traumatic events that have shaped human history, but only one event, the birth of Christ, the birth of a small child, still serves to be that historic demarcation point or date that time was changed from BC to AD. For my family, that day of demarcation was our house fire. The day we lost everything but gained much more.

Everything we have done or owned is thought of as happened or possessed either pre or post fire. Occasions, such as looking for a particular saw that I had and needed for a project; after searching high and low for it, I then remember, oh yes, I had that saw before the fire. Or, when was the last time we went to visit Aunt Liz? Oh, that was a year before the fire.

It is amazing how the human mind works to put such an event as such a powerful, emblazoned place marker of time that really defines actions into two stages of time or life. The fire experience was one of those types of events that runs one through the complete gamut of emotions – from highs to lows; from tears of sadness to tears of joy.

In Jimmy Valvano's 1993 ESPN ESPY Arthur Ash Award acceptance speech, he said, *"Three things that each person should do every day – 1. Laugh, 2. Think, spend some time in thought, 3. Have your emotions moved to tears. To laugh, think and cry, that is a full day. That is a heck of a day. If you do that 7 days a week, you will have something special."* Jimmy at that time was in his last days of life with terminal cancer spread throughout his body, providing us with words of wisdom from a dying man heading to meet his Maker.

Well, our fire story was something special. I was able to laugh because my family was spared unhurt. I was able to contemplate the event and events from the subsequent days and weeks to see and experience a little of God's plan in action. My emotions were moved to tears first seeing the destruction, especially in the upstairs bedrooms where we all slept until being miraculously woken up, and the feeling of the human tragedy spared us by the Lord, but mainly from tears of joy realizing what was going on and the feeling of being part of God's plan to bring the Holy Spirit into action to the community surrounding me. As Jimmy said above, that was something special.

I will never know why the Lord picked me, my family or why he picked my neighborhood, my parish of St. Lawrence or the Castleton/Lawrence Townships in northeastern Indianapolis. I am not sure if the people in this area were in particular disarray needing a spiritual pick me up. St. Francis of Assisi once said, *"I have been all things unholy. If God can work through me, He can work through anyone."* Not only can He, but He did. What I witnessed was a complete transformation of the people I came into contact with. A collection of normal people moved to charity and by love. A bunch of normal people filled with the Holy Spirit. They reminded me of the description in the Acts of the Apostles documenting the Spirit fullness of the early Church; the fervor of love, joy and charity that was thrust upon them as they were filled by the Holy Spirit[3]. Their zeal for community building, based on the left lung of Jesus' commands to attain salvation, unconditional love and compassion for one's neighbor, was the essence, the engine fueling the beginning of Jesus' Church. *"Go, therefore, and make disciples of all nations."*[4]

I will never know if or how long the spiritual transformation of those touched by these events lasted. One can observe past events, such as the terrorist attack on the World Trade Center in New York City on September 11, 2001, where directly afterward, there was a rush to spirituality, to pray for the victims as well as to get a spiritual hold on what had just happened. Later, after spirituality in this country built to a peak about a month after this horrific event, as time marched on, the spiritual level could be seen and felt trending back downward. Now, in 2015 I am sorry to say, the spiritual meter in the United States is even lower now than it was prior to the event.

---

[3] Acts 2:42-47
[4] Matthew 28:19

I am sure a similar phenomenon happened for the community surrounding us in the weeks and years after the fire. Some may not even remember the event anymore, but for that shining moment in Camelot, the Spirit of the Lord was shining and churning a Divine fire of discipleship and mercy. A fire that raged through the various communities touched by the event, that showed what a community filled with the Lord and the Holy Spirit looks like, feels like and works like. And I am sure that in some way the event has emblazoned an indelible mark of some kind that continues to bring each one closer to God and His Salvation.

This event was, "the best thing to ever happen to me that I would not wish on my worst enemy". It was so traumatic yet so spiritually invigorating that it remains to this day as the most forming experience in my life. Just the fact that my family and I survived this ordeal is a testimony that our work here is not finished for the Lord and maybe he just wanted me to write this book to tell His story to the world; to give my readers a glimpse of how Jesus can work and should work in our lives. A story that documents that bad things can happen and bring about good. So, have peace when trials befall you. The fire experience, as given to my family by Jesus, has challenged me to tell the story ever since the day it happened. As a part of writing that story, I realized that I owe the Lord all things. I do not deserve or am entitled to anything. All that I am and have are gifts from the Lord and need to be lived and celebrated in that manner.

I also discovered the value and the responsibility to giving back to the Lord. After receiving the multitude of gifts from my surrounding community after the fire, it awakened my sense of the importance to give of one's self, not as a debt repayment gesture but solely out of unconditional love. 1 John 4:8 he says, *"God is love"*. When we are disciples and do works out of love, we are thus doing God's works. In the days and weeks after the fire, I was able to see God's works in the people that surrounded our family. I was challenged from that point to give back to my surrounding society with unconditional love. Give until it hurts – or burns.

When you are in a situation where you have lost all your worldly goods and are virtually homeless, that tears you down to your personal essence. Seeing the Spiritual revitalization of my community and the joy of having my family with me unharmed, it became a daunting task to not only pick up the pieces to rebuild our lives but also coming to grips with what the Lord had in mind for my family and me. With all the trauma and events that transpired starting in the early morning hours of July 5, 1996, what did the Lord now want from us? We were spared for a reason. As stated in Luke 12:48, the Lord said, *"Much will be required of the person entrusted with much, and still more will be demanded of the person entrusted with more."* Now being the recipient of the biggest possible gift, the whole family surviving and experiencing the fire episode unscathed, I had a feeling that "much" and even "more" was indeed given, therefore, I needed to figure out how and what the Lord had in mind for me. Much would be demanded.

So, I have no idea why God picked me. I was not a high profile person of means, nor was I a poor person on the streets. I was somewhat active in my social groups and church parish (St. Lawrence, Indianapolis, IN), but could hardly be dubbed as a church or community leader. I guess you could have called me an average Joe and family fitting the same category as well. For some reason, God chose my family and me to energize his people in northeastern Indianapolis.

At the time of the fire, I was a 40-year-old husband and father of three lovely children – Emily 12, Steven 9 and Elizabeth 7 - and married to my best friend and wife Cathy. We went to church every Sunday. The three children all attended St Lawrence Catholic elementary school. All were good students, but none were in the "in" crowd, nor were any of them tabbed to be on the Religious Vocation watch list.

As far as extracurricular activities, Cathy was a Girl Scout leader for our girls. Cathy had been a scout leader for 4 years. Her Girl Scout group was made up of girls from the St. Lawrence School. Cathy also taught $2^{nd}$ grade at Grassy Creek Elementary school in Warren Township.

I was Steven's assistant Cub Scout Den leader for a year. Boys in the Cub pack were also from St. Lawrence School. I volunteered as soccer coaches for several years coaching the three kids' soccer teams. I also volunteered and served as a soccer league director in the local youth soccer association that year. At St. Lawrence, I served for one season as the girls' basketball coach. So, as you can see, both Cathy and I were active but not world beaters – we still had free time.

Now, as far as spirituality, again, my family went to Mass weekly. I would characterize myself as a good Catholic but not totally formed in my Catholic faith. At church, I was one of the invisible members in the congregation that came on time and raced to get out of the parking lot before the traffic jam.

I was not a Bible reader nor was I really inclined to investigate my faith at that time. For instance, there was one car ride where another Protestant coworker and I were heading to an out of town plant location in a car together. He started asking me questions about the Catholic Faith. First, he caught me by surprise, but I was totally unable to provide any apologetically astute response at all to his questions. That was embarrassing. But I really failed do anything more about it at the time.

The one motivating thing for me was my three children. I felt the need to get more active and knowledgeable in my Catholic Faith so I could pass that Faith on to them. So I began to at least contemplate what I needed to do to get more in tune with the Catholic Church and what She teaches.

The Book of Proverbs says, *"Many are the plans of the human heart, but it is the decision of the Lord that endures"*[5]. The Lord started to prepare me for what He had in mind. I had no idea what was to come and went on my merry way planning my life and making my way as Frank Sinatra sang "doing it my way", so I thought.

God's ways are not man's ways. He does surprising things – even shocking things – with the least expected and qualified person. Just

---

[5] Proverbs 19:21

look at Jesus' birth – poor carpenter family. Not on anyone's radar screen. The world changed 33 years later though because of this poor carpenter's child.

Again, I do not know why the Lord picked our family. That is something that I am sure I will find out, God willing, when I go to meet my Maker in Heaven. Just the same, my family was chosen and His will was done through us – whether I was ready or not.

Pope Saint John Paul II said this, *"Have no fear of moving into the unknown. Simply step out fearlessly knowing that I am with you, therefore no harm can befall you; all is very, very well. Do this in complete faith and confidence."* Sometimes when God calls, it is time to fearlessly step out. And doing so having unfailing faith in God that all this will be worth it in the end and the world will be a better place, one way or another, because of our small sacrifice. I may not ever see the fruits or be in a place to recognize the fruits of this labor of love, but I know that it has and probably is still making an impact on the participants of the Fire Story.

## Part 1: The Best Thing That Ever Happened To Me That I Would Not Wish On My Worst Enemy

This first part of the book chronicles the years and days before, during and after our house fire on July 5, 1996. It chronicles Spiritual struggles, Spiritual rebirth, and Spiritual revelations. This section documents how the Lord developed and implemented his plan through my family to energize, at least as far as I know, the local groups of people that my family touched and came into contact with. It also chronicles the many gifts that my family and especially I received over that one year beginning with the fire. When pondering the gifts received from Jesus throughout the fire story, many of the worldly population of today would disagree with my assessment that losing one's worldly possessions would constitute a good gift. Some may outright think I am even loony for saying these gifts are not really afflictions. I give you now the story chronicling the "Best thing that ever happened to me that I would not wish on my worst enemy".

Part 1 Chapters

Chapter 2: Life Prior To The Fire

Chapter 3: The Fire: 7-4-96 to 7-12-96

Pictures From The House After The Fire

Chapter 4: The Reality Sets In - Getting Life Restarted Again

Chapter 5: The Face Of Angels

## Chapter 2: Life Prior To The Fire

I have always had a spiritual side from childhood on up. At one time, I thought that I was going to be a Priest. I remember playing Priest, saying my pretend Mass in the basement of my boyhood home on East Ashman Street in Midland, Michigan. I always felt a closeness to God when I attended daily (in grade school) and weekly Mass. I was an Altar Boy from age 8 to high school.

I soon gave up my Priestly aspirations in high school and went on to Michigan State University. At the beginning of my college career, I maintained my Faith traditions, but peer pressure and laziness crept in and I started to lax off on my weekly Mass duty. I decided to sleep in instead. Luckily that only lasted about one term (MSU at that time was on a 4 term school cycle, 3 months each) but it was probably the worst three months of my life.

I was not sure at that time what was missing. My classes were extremely tough that winter term and I was scraping to just pass any of them. My whole demeanor had changed. I was not happy. I started to get involved with the party scene. The more I tried to find an even road to run, the darker my soul felt.

The next spring term, things started to change for the better. John 14:17 says, *"I will not leave you as orphans."* First, I made the decision to faithfully go back to weekly Mass. The retransformation was amazing. It was as if a sheet was removed from over me. *"Immediately things like scales fell from his eyes and he regained his sight."*[6] Reminiscent of Saul's conversion, my whole demeanor again changed back to one of joy and peace. I was bewildered why I thought sleeping in on Sundays was going to be so great in the first place. I never missed a Sunday Mass for the rest of my college career.

The second thing that happened the following year, I began going out with and dating my now wife Cathy. If you asked her, it was her

---

[6] Acts 9:18 Saul's conversion and Baptism

influence that caused my spiritual rebirth, but really that had already started. Cathy did have a profound effect on the depth of my spiritual experience, because now I had someone to go to church with. I had someone who showed me what true love was. Cathy's love helped me come to closer grips with the deep love that God had for me.

Cathy and I were married in 1979 and started our new chapter of life together. Again, we went to weekly Mass together and had a feeling of spirituality, but I would say we really did not reach for that brass ring to celebrate and share our Faith with the world. As stated in the prior chapter, my spiritual life was basically going through the motions with the feeling that attending Mass every Sunday fulfilled my Catholic obligations. I was the equivalent to a Catholic couch potato. I left the discipleship and the real religious stuff to the Priests and the Sisters. I was a good guy. Tried to make good decisions per my Faith. I tried to obey the 10 Commandments. I was good, right?

The second part of God's plan fell into place when I found a job in Indianapolis with RCA (TV) and we moved to Indianapolis. Although we would move out and back again prior to the fire, we really enjoyed living in Indianapolis.

Now on Cathy's side, she had a difficult transition to life in Indianapolis. Coming from the big city, Detroit, and making the big move away from the family right after we were married, was tough. Everything was small to Cathy at first. Indianapolis was huge to me (grew up in Midland, MI, population of about 30,000). To her, Indianapolis was tiny. Even the Sunday paper was tiny compared to Detroit's. It was difficult even for me weathering the corn and herbicide commercials on TV. The coup-de-grace happened when Cathy switched from the Indianapolis school system to teach in Warren Township – a suburb of Indianapolis. Her new school, Grassy Creek, was in the middle of a corn field and almost too much to handle for a Metro Detroit girl. She got over it and soon was a passionate and loving Indy girl.

God started to creep into my life more as time went on – and creep is a good word for it. The first of my revelations happened after our children were born. I began to contemplate how I was going to pass on my religion to them and what would they believe. I definitely wanted them to grow up and stay Catholic. My kids' future Faith situation started me thinking that I myself needed to get serious about my Faith, so I could pass it on to my kids. You cannot teach what you do not know.

The first thing that I did was to start to get involved with my kid's activities – soccer, scouts. My dad, when I was growing up, was a great role model and prolifically volunteered for charities and other ministries of the church and the city (e.g. ran for and served as a Midland City Councilman for two terms). The problem was, he was frequently gone evenings doing his volunteer work and I missed having him around. For this reason, I resigned that when I became an adult with children, I would be involved in volunteer work to give back to the world, but I would concentrate on efforts that involved my kids, such as coaching sports teams, being a Scout leader etc. My volunteer work started my discipleship growth but did not really translate to a Faith and love of God growth yet.

My next spiritual jolt came at my dad's funeral in 1992. Of course, losing a parent is traumatic and world changing. By losing my dad, I lost someone that I could call on the phone anytime and get advice or just talk about what was happening in my life. Losing a dad is akin to cutting loose one of your safety nets. The moment that mesmerized me though was at the gravesite. As people started to head back to their cars, my Aunt Liz (dad's mother's younger sister) started to sing Amazing Grace. Hearing her sing, caused me to be frozen there in place motionless and numb. I was captivated. I felt as if I was standing on a cloud floating above the ground watching this enormous showing of Faith and love.

St Francis once said, *"We should seek not so much to pray but to become prayer"*. This experience of one person glorifying God with a joyful and faith filled display in the eyes of sorrow and death elevated my spiritual senses. I could not move. I was sucked into Aunt Liz's glorious and passionate prayer. I felt as if I was a stationary pole with a camera filming the event as people walked by. It seemed as if the only two people not moving in the universe were Aunt Liz and me. I was fixated on the face of Jesus that was my Aunt Liz celebrating the passing of my dad hopefully up to Heaven. I did not know it at the time, but I was suspended in time within and participating in Aunt Liz's prayer. A prayer of thanksgiving for the gift of my dad's life in her life.

That event did make a change in my life and my spirituality. Although it was an event that I thought about daily – how I felt and how my spiritual inner being was boiling *("Were not our hearts burning [within us] while he spoke to us on the way and opened the scriptures to us?"[7])*, it really was not until my CRHP (Christ Renews His Parish, pronounced Chirp) retreat where the fire that was simmering in my soul and God's mighty hand finally came together to really rock my world. I went through my daily life constantly thinking of that event at the grave site, trying to reconcile what it meant in my life. I wrestled with the memory. It was tugging at me, poking me to let God in; to throw the nets away and follow. Jesus' invitation resembled St. Peter's called by the angel in his cell in Acts 12:7, *"Suddenly the angel of the Lord stood by him and a light shone in the cell. He tapped Peter on the side and awakened him, saying, 'Get up quickly'"*. I was being "tapped" by Jesus. I just needed a little bigger nudge to get up and walk out of my cell.

About 5-6 years leading up to my decision to finally sign up for a CRHP weekend retreat, my parents and several relatives also made their CRHP retreats. All came back and told glowingly wonderful stories trying to describe how Spirit filled the retreat was and that I had to make a CRHP weekend myself.

I was less than attentive to their glorious descriptions. I wrote it off to over zealousness and filed the conversations in the back of my mind. I since discovered that their inability to energize me with their description of the wonders of the retreat was not due to any lack of actual wonder experienced. It really was a clear case that there were

---

[7] Luke 24:32

no human words or ways to express how wonderful and Spirit filled the retreat actually was.

Perhaps it was my Aunt Liz's graveside prayer that drew me or perhaps Jesus' nudge above finally escalated to a push or shove. Finally, in the fall of 1995 I decided to sign up for that CRHP weekend at my then parish, St. Lawrence. I do not remember what caused the light bulb to turn on. I sure did not know and was not prepared for the effect the weekend would have on my life both spiritually and physically.

The Christ Renews His Parish program is divided into two retreats. First, the participants from the prior retreat present the CRHP retreat to my group. Part 2, volunteers from my retreat group next meet and form a team that presents the series of talks and events for the next CRHP retreat group six months later. So, other than the Mass that is said during the retreat, the entire retreat program is put on by lay people. It is a powerful event for both receiving and presenting teams. Fellow parishioners that you sit with in the pews every week in church are now staring you in the face giving their Faith journeys and challenging you to embrace Jesus to become a full on disciple of His.

When the formation process begins for the second retreat, you really come to grips with where your Faith journey lies. The level of Faith that you are now preparing to share with the new group of men really challenges you to walk the walk. You cannot teach it if you do not actually believe it. During the actual retreat, you get the immense feeling of the power of the Holy Spirit flowing through your veins as His words spill out of your mouth and embed into your audience's hearts.

So, in the fall, I check in for my first CRHP weekend early Saturday morning at the Indianapolis Diocese's retreat house and was shown to my room that I would be sleeping in. The retreat house was a beautiful place. The building accommodations were modest but comfortable. The grounds were pretty, wooded, with flower bed prayer trails that one could walk and spend time with the Lord in prayer.

The retreat was spiritually mesmerizing even more than promised. As stated before, it is one of those turning point adventures that one cannot explain because there are not words that can be used to fully grasp what had happened to me and how this weekend worked to energize my Faith and Spirituality. I cannot go into detail about the individual parts from the retreat that were so uplifting, because if you have not been on a CRHP retreat, well you will just have to experience that for yourself. If you have already, I am sure I do not need to go into any detail for you. To suffice, as quoted in the last chapter by Jimmy Valvano, it was a heck of a weekend, something really special. We laughed. We were in deep thought and pondered the Lord's words we were hearing from our fellow CRHP brother presenters. Our emotions were brought to tears. The Holy Spirit was definitely present. He enveloped our beings that weekend and raised us up to a new closeness to Him that I had never encountered before.

The second phase of CRHP was even more spiritually uplifting. I was deeply moved and surprised that another retreat experience could top the initial CRHP weekend, but the second half of CRHP sent me up the rest of the way up the holy mountain. What I didn't know at the time was Jesus was preparing me for what He had in mind only a few months in the future. He was preparing me spiritually to accept His call for a piece of work He had planned for me. He knew the cross that He was asking me to carry would be a tough one so He needed to prop me up, analogous to sending me to the spiritual gym, to be able to withstand what He had planned for me and family.

So, the second phase of CRHP started. The 10 members for the 1996 spring CRHP presenting team met weekly over the six months after our initial retreat that then lead up to the upcoming spring retreat. It was amazing. As we met, I could feel the spiritual energy rising from meeting to meeting within our group. The CRHP process has a teaching manual that walked us through and prepared us to put on the event. The CRHP training itself is reminiscent of a spiritual exercise program to build up our closeness to Jesus and build us up as disciples then capable to go out to this next group of men and bring the Word of God to them.

# I Have Come To Set The Earth On Fire

The process was totally and unexpectedly amazing. As the months progressed, when the 10 of us met, our spirituality during the meeting seemed to take off like a nuclear reaction. As we delved into our lesson for the week, we could feel the Spiritual energy in the room and within us build and start to swirl within the room. Through the formation process, we began to feel empowered by the Holy Spirit to step out of our comfort zones to spread the Word of God to the world as true disciples. Every meeting someone would share an encounter they had the prior week sharing God with a friend, family member or some random passerby. *"The seventy [-two] returned rejoicing, and said, 'Lord, even the demons are subject to us because of your name.'"*[8] I remember shaking my head on several occasions where a member did something that sounded way outside that person's comfort zone. The outcomes as recanted by the individuals were always uplifting and successful. Each act of discipleship inspired the rest of us to leave our comfort zones and do something, be a disciple for the Lord.

It was during this formation time that the Lord started to up his game with me and started to get me involved with his upcoming planned event. As part of the CRHP formation, we had homework to do and read. I had a period of time after Cathy and the kids went to bed where I had about an hour to spend on my reading and prep for the next week's formation training meeting when the house was nice and quiet and peaceful. Almost immediately after starting this regimen, I felt filled with the Holy Spirit as I was sitting on my Lay-Z-Boy rocker reading the lesson. So much so that I was frequently overcome by my feelings which interrupted what I was reading. There were times when I was compelled to get off my chair and kneel down because I strongly felt the presence of Jesus in my midst. There were times when I actually did fall to my knees.

When these periods of the presence of the Holy Spirit happened, I began entering into deep contemplation prayer modes. I would clear my mind of all distractions and start to ask and listen to what I felt the

---

[8] Luke 10:17

Lord was trying to convey to me. In a homily that St. Pope John Paul II gave on January 15, 1995, he said,

> "Do not be slow to answer the Lord's call!...First he provokes a new awareness of his presence – the Burning Bush. When we begin to show an interest, he calls us by name. When our answer becomes specific and like Moses, we say: 'Here I am', then he reveals more clearly both himself and his compassionate love for his people in need. Gradually he leads us to discover the practical way in which we should serve him: 'I will send you.' And usually it is then that fears and doubts come to disturb us and make it more difficult to decide. It is then that we need to hear the Lord's assurance: 'I am with you'".

How prophetic these words from St. Pope John Paul II were. That is down to the word how God's call that I encountered really came to fruition.

Initially I did not receive any instructions, or the plan laid out for me. The Lord gave me messages that He loved me, and every prayer discussion session always ended with a deep, cleansing feeling of peace. A peace that I have not felt before or since. That was the extent. I knew this was extraordinary in itself and was glad that the Lord was giving me these encouraging messages and the lovely feeling of peace, but in the same vein was confused as to why this was happening.

After a week of the simple "I love you" messages, the Lord started to up the ante so to speak. In my meditative prayer, He started to give me messages that something bad was going to happen. That was all. This time was so special because I remember dialoguing with God asking what was going to happen. When do you get a chance to actually converse with God?! I got the feeling that whatever it was, it was going to be something pretty traumatic. I remember asking if this "something bad to happen" would include someone from my family getting hurt or losing them. I did get the answer that, "All would be ok. Wait and believe."

A quote of Thomas Aquinas taken from Peter Kreeft's book on St. Thomas Aquinas read like this, *"Therefore, we can trust God for everything, as if everything is His predestinating providence, for everything really is His providence."*[9] I felt comfort knowing I and my family were in God's hands and that was a special place to be. St. John Paul II stated, *"Do not be afraid...Put out into the deep and let down your nets for a catch"*. That is exactly my feeling going forward. The Lord had a plan involving my family and me. All I had to do was throw the nets out and Jesus would take care of the rest.

This same message was conveyed to me every night for a little over a month. The discussion I had with the Lord was always the same. "Prepare, something will happen to your family. You will all be unharmed." Then came the gift and feeling of total cleansing peace. Again, it is hard to describe the feeling of total peace given. It is another one of those feelings and emotions that there are no earthly words to describe. I have wondered since that time, when I hear someone talking about peace and wanting to have peace, what they are really aiming for? One thing that I learned from this experience, was peace cannot be earned. Peace is given – by the Almighty Lord – as a supreme gift. One cannot put together a plan and execute an action to arrive at total peace.

Then, after about six weeks of these meditation sessions, the messages ended. I guess the Lord felt that he had built me up sufficiently to weather what was to come. Mother Teresa once said, *"I know God won't give me anything I can't handle. I just wish he didn't trust me so much"*. This was the blind faith that I had to bring forward. I was given no indication on what or when this event was going to happen. The Bible says the same thing pertaining the timing for the end of the world. Don't waste time trying to predict when it will happen. When it happens it happens.

---

[9] Peter Kreeft, Practical Theology, Spiritual Direction from St. Thomas Aquinas

# I Have Come To Set The Earth On Fire

Now a couple of things perplexed me after these message events ended and even after the fire happened. In general, why did I not tell anyone, especially Cathy, of what I was hearing from God? To that, I do not know. I am usually one that is free and want to keep people informed and discuss momentous events - of which none could be more momentous than a discussion with the Almighty. God put in me peace of mind that I was not supposed to let on to anyone about His plan. It was not a specific statement or instruction received, it was just implied, just the way the main message itself was conveyed. I just knew it was God's will that I not discuss this with anyone. What would I say anyway? I did not know the time or date. I really did not even know what the event itself was to be. The Lord really gave me nothing I could pass on with any credibility.

The second question I asked myself was, "Was that real?" Was it just my mind playing tricks? Was I in love with the idea of talking to God as happened in the Biblical stories of Abraham, Noah and Moses? Was there some other spiritual being trying to communicate with me, possibly one not with my best interests in mind? The key to answer those questions was the constant ending of each prayer session with the deep feeling of peace. That convinced me my sessions and discussions were real and were truly from Jesus. Now whether I was actually talking with Jesus or an angel or possibly even the Lord sent someone like my departed dad to give the messages, I will not know that until I hopefully reap my just rewards.

My CRHP formation then came to a close. The Lord's messages to me were always present in my mind and soul, but as the spring CRHP retreat came to fruition, the retreat became my main focus. We all had our parts that we discerned, and I think we each ended up with the job that most touched us during our initial CRHP retreat. At least that is true for my job at the retreat. I did not have one of the speaking parts, but I can say that I had the most important position there. For the ones that have made a CRHP retreat, my position was the one responsible for the event that moved the retreaters' emotions to tears (of joy that is). Those of you CRHP alumni will know exactly what job I am referring to. I also was a table discussion leader which was a great spiritual lift in itself.

As I said earlier, the second CRHP weekend was even more uplifting than the first. Seeing the new CRHP participants have their "heck of a weekend". Seeing them laugh, ponder Christ, and yes, emotions moved to tears. It made me feel so Spiritually uplifted watching the new men turn from guys off the street into flaming disciples. That was something special.

The high point for me was the Mass that Saturday evening. I have never felt so joyous and Spirit filled in celebration of the Eucharist as I did that day, that Mass. The high point for me at the Mass was just after the Our Father Prayer. At that time, all the men from the formation team were standing behind the altar with our hands still clasped. When we all spoke the words, "For the Kingdom, the Power and the Glory are Yours, now and forever", we all raised our hands as is the normal custom. I was so filled with the Spirit that my hands shot straight up, with my two CRHP brothers on either side's hands, straight up to Heaven. I was so juiced with the Spirit that I could not hold back. I wanted to explode, and reaching up as high as I could was the best I could manage to express to the Lord how I felt; how grateful I was; what a privilege it was, and how blessed I was to be standing there on the altar with my CRHP brothers after six months of meeting, praying, laughing and crying together, building up to this very moment now in total praise and worship of God and His infinite glory.

It was not until really today that what happened at this Mass really sunk in. Earlier this week, I was listening to the EWTN radio station as I was driving. The program was a prerecorded talk that Fr. Larry Richards gave to a group of men at his parish in Erie, PA. In that presentation, he was talking about the Mass. He said that the reason the Mass is so glorious is that when we are celebrating Mass, earth meets Heaven. We are sharing Heaven with Jesus, the angels and the Saints while we are celebrating the Mass. At the time hearing this, my reaction when hearing Fr. Larry's statement was, "Come on Father Larry, Mass does not feel like Heaven to me. I feel close to Jesus but I am sure Heaven is a bit more joyous and a lot more intensely praising God."

Still it did not hit me until today at a men's Bible study. One of the men, George, recounted a similar super Spiritual Mass encounter he had during a retreat. That was it! Suddenly it clicked. The reason George and I had felt so spiritually alive at these Masses, was, we were indeed in Heaven worshiping the presence of Jesus! So now the question is, why can't I be that exhilarated and joyously praising God at every Mass? That is my quest. As my friend from Bible study experienced, we both climbed up to the summit of the mountain. We had been in Heaven. The fire now burns for more of the same. That Mass experience felt so good and wonderful I want that every Mass!

I did not want that Mass to ever end – well, technically the Mass never does end – but you know what I mean. As Peter said to Jesus at the Transfiguration, *"Lord, it is good that we are here. If you wish, I will make three tents."*[10] Just as Peter, I would have done anything to make that high moment last. I felt a sense of impending loss. I knew if I went down off of the mountain, out from Heaven, that I probably would have difficulty, or ever at all, to get all the way back up there. But as Jesus, in his Godly wisdom, ushered the three Apostles back down the mountain, because they had a big job ahead of them to energize the world about Jesus, His Resurrection and to build His Church. I had the same command to go back down the mountain. Just as the Apostles did not understand that in a few weeks, they would be thrust into God's holy business, I also had no idea that, in a short while, I too was going to be a part of God's plan to energize, at least my part of the world.

Who knows? I think there was so much spiritual energy that weekend that there was a little miracle that happened toward downtown Indianapolis. The Indianapolis Pacers were playing the New York Nicks in a basketball playoff game at Market Square Arena that Sunday afternoon as well. Just before the end of the retreat, the Pacers were losing by 6 points with 9 seconds to go for their playoff game with the New York Nicks. Reggie Miller pulled off a most miraculous feat scoring 8 points in the final 9 seconds of that game to win that playoff game. Too bad CRHP did not continue through the

---

[10] Mat 17:4

rest of the week because the Pacers ended up needing a few more miracles and ended up losing the series.

Time went on and the memory of the messages given waned a bit. The messages were always in the back of my mind because I always wondered when this thing was going to happen; if it was going to happen. A second validation occurred in mid-June. One day Cathy came to me and said Elizabeth, our then youngest, had received some message that something was going to happen and would I talk to her. WOW! I got the biggest, glowing smile on my face and pulled Elizabeth aside and confidently assured her not worry that we would all be ok. I was amazed that someone else was given the same premonition of the impending happening. Again, there was no date given so neither Liz nor I had any thought on when this storm would blow through our family.

One thing that Jesus kept in my life after CRHP was a love for the Mass. I think he was trying to keep me engaged and ready when the time came for me to endure my cross He had planned for me and that I would be there for my family when it happened. I tried to go to Mass every chance that I could, meaning Saturday mornings along with Sunday celebrations. Mass to me was just that, a celebration. I felt the energy of the Risen Lord in the church – similarly to the Heavenly feeling I received during that last CRHP Mass. I could feel His glory emanating from each of the persons attending the Mass. I could feel God's love. The Mass came alive as soon as the Priest entered. The Epistle and Gospel readings along with the Priest's sermons all seemed were talking directly at me. I could feel God's presence crescendo as the Consecration completed. I was truly seeing the Body, Blood, Soul and Divinity of our Lord and Savior. Communion was the high point in my day. I felt warm and Spiritually empowered as the host and wine were being consumed. After the final greeting to "Go in Peace" I was ready to take on the world. I could not wait until I had the chance to go again.

I have so much to thank my Guardian Angel. Over the next two months I think he put in a little overtime to keep me first out of harm's way, then to keep me fully grounded in what the Lord was preparing me for. Mother Teresa once said, *"Never travel faster than your Guardian Angel can fly"*. I think the Lord fit my Angel with a set of super strength, high speed wings.

## Chapter 3: The Fire: 7-4-96 to 7-12-96

*"The LORD is my shepherd; there is nothing I lack. In green pastures he makes me lie down; to still waters he leads me; he restores my soul. He guides me along right paths for the sake of his name. Even though I walk through the valley of the shadow of death, I will fear no evil, for you are with me; your rod and your staff comfort me.*

*"You set a table before me in front of my enemies; You anoint my head with oil; my cup overflows. Indeed, goodness and mercy will pursue me all the days of my life; I will dwell in the house of the LORD for endless days."*[11]

July 4th,1996 was no different than 4th of July days before. There were parades, picnics, cook outs and fireworks. There were no warning signs pointing to anything of danger lurking in the near future. *"But of that day and hour no one knows..."*[12] Just as the end of the world, Jesus does not make known to us humans when He plans to spring these little life changing events. We were not aware then, but the real fireworks were yet to come.

The evening of the 4th, our family met up with the neighbors from across the street, the Crawfords, to go out for a picnic cook out in the country and a few fireworks besides. The Crawford's two boys were best friends with my son Steven and we all had a good time. The weather was pleasant. We all enjoyed the evening and the holiday festivities.

We returned home, and all went to bed as normal at about 11:00. So far, all normal and good. That changed about 2:00am a few hours later. God's plan had started to hatch.

---

[11] Psalm 23:1-6
[12] Matthew 24:36

Luckily, Cathy was sleeping a bit restlessly because she had a little heartburn caused by the grilled cookout food from earlier in the evening. Then Steven got up to go to the bathroom, something that he rarely, if ever, had done in the past. So, when Steven rustled into the bathroom, the clatter woke Cathy up from her restless sleep. At this point, I was soundly asleep.

Cathy noticed an odd smell and woke me up to investigate. When awakened, there was a faint but noticeable smell similar to rubber or plastic burning. At the time, the smell, of course, was out of place but I had no other evidence of a fire close by (heat, smoke etc.) or feelings that danger lurked just a matter of feet away. Because the smell was out of place, first I had to officially confirm this smell did not pose any danger to the family and secondly, the curiosity in me had to put a place to the smell. I got up in my sleeping attire (t-shirt and underwear) to pursue the origin of this burning smell.

Now, our house was located next to a small swatch of common ground from our subdivision which ran along a busy street, so our house was in close proximity to the street. There were periodic accidents or people with car trouble on the main road, so my first thought was the smell came from a car overheating that was parked on the street. The smell resembled that type of odor – the rubber smell of hoses from a car's coolant system when the car overheats.

I looked out from our 2$^{nd}$ story window of our bedroom, which looked out toward the street, but saw no signs of any car or any car in distress. So, I started to walk the house, sniffing as I went, to try to pin point the origin of the odor. First, I walked the upstairs and seemed that the odor was lessening rather than building. Next to be inspected was the down stairs. After walking and sniffing throughout the downstairs, there was really no signs of anything amiss. I checked the stove and oven, all were turned off. All seemed normal. No signs of anything bad. No odors detected in the downstairs either that gave me any cause for concern.

I still had this feeling in the pit of my stomach that there was something wrong. Other than the faint char odor, there were no other clues for danger; not even any feel of any heat or essence of any smoke. I kept telling myself that all was OK because there would have at least been some sort of sensation of a heat gradient somewhere if the smoke smell was coming from somewhere in our house. The feeling I had persisted. Perhaps it was the Lord prodding me to keep going because He promised me that my family would be unharmed.

I then got the urge to check the garage. Again, there was no reason to believe there was any danger or the origin of a fire behind that door to the garage; no heat, not even any sense of increased odor as the door was approached. The garage was just the last place yet to be checked and cleared. The door to the garage from the house opened into our family room. Above the garage was an attic where we had random things stored, including archive teaching supplies and old bulletin board decorations, etc. The attic above the garage formed the north wall of the Master bedroom where Cathy and I were sleeping.

Despite the lack of evidence, I had a premonition that there was something amiss in the garage. I grabbed the handle of the garage door, then remembered one fire safety lesson taught if investigating a house fire. Before gaining access to a room with a closed door, touch the door handle with the back of your hand first to confirm it is not hot before grabbing to turn. Well, I was fortunate that the handle felt normal and was not hot, but remember thinking, "that was a dumb thing to do".

When the door to the garage was opened, I received a big shock! The whole ceiling of the garage was a blaze. I did not know how long it had been since the fire started but it was definitely time to get out and fast! My first inclination was, should I hop in and drive the cars out because the ceiling above them was ablaze and they would certainly be lost? This was my first exposure to give up my possessions. They were not worth the risk and there were much more important things to do at that time, such as to get my family out of this now burning house. The cars at that point did not matter – thank God.

Now, leading up to this point and when the door to the garage was opened, I had, as mentioned above, a feeling something was wrong, even though no hard evidence presented itself until the door to the garage was in fact opened. I felt that there was some disturbance going on. It was a weird feeling; a feeling of somewhat disbelief that something bad could or should be happening. Even when the door to the garage was fully open and the flames in the ceiling became totally visible, there was a brief moment of feeling that, "this could not be real". This type of thing only happens on TV. The feeling puts you in a strange place, kind of levitation between reality and the clouds of disbelief. I felt caught, floating between the two. I had to make a quick decision though. First to open that door. It is one of those feelings, a premonition something is bad behind that door, but maybe not. If I do not open the door, maybe it's nothing or it will go away. So, the first hurdle was cleared when I decided to open the door. The second decision came when seeing the flames to cognately determine the flames were real. The initial feeling, granted I was just awakened from a deep sleep, was, "Man, this has to be a bad dream. This is not really happening." After that fleeting moment of doubt was over, it was time to go spring into action.

Immediately I ran up the stairs yelling to Cathy and the kids to wake up and get out of the house. At the top of the stairs, as I was running up the stairs to get everyone out, I saw Cathy jumping out of bed and running to get the kids out. Emily (the oldest) and Steven awoke and passed me on the stairs in their exit down the stairs. Cathy whisked by, down the hall, heading for Liz's room. Before I reached the top of the stairs, Cathy, carrying Liz, passed me heading down the stairs and out the front door. It was a good thing that we had worked on a fire exit plan in months before with the kids, so all knew to exit the house and go to our neighbor's house across the street, which was the same family that we celebrated the 4th with the evening before.

As my family was exiting down the stairs and out the front door, there still was no real evidence inside of the house of the fire as of yet. Again, no feeling of any heat from the fire, no smoke either. The exit path from the upstairs down to the front door was completely free of any danger or any signs of danger. God had fulfilled his first promise to me. No one was injured. It was also a blessing that the kids did not have to endure any real trauma of seeing any flames as they exited because the flames were still completely contained within the garage and attic at that time. That gave me my first point of solace that morning. In view of all the trauma going on and danger lurking, the realization hit. This definitely could have been much worse. I could see all five or our Guardian Angels hard at work, doing Jesus' beckoning.

After my family had exited, I was still upstairs making sure all were out of the house, making my count – 1, 2, 3, 4 good all were out. We also had 2 cats, so attempted to find the cats to get them out to safety, but was not successful. They were hiding somewhere. I knew my time was limited and had to execute my exit. The fire had not yet broken through any walls yet, so felt I had a few more seconds, went into our bedroom and put on a pair of shorts. That turned out to be a smart thing as time would tell. I knew I did not have much time, so the pair of shorts was the last thing grabbed before heading down the stairs. I did pick up one more thing though as I exited, the cordless phone so I could call 911.

After exiting the house, my first task was to wake the next-door neighbors and get them out from their house safely. Their house was located on the East side of our house. The subdivision house plotting layout was what was called a Zero Lot Line, so the houses were close together and knew there was a significant risk for fire to spread to their house. Luckily there were no houses on the other sides (west and south) because the subdivision park and common grounds wrapped around our house giving plenty of space to prevent any fire spread in those other directions. After ringing their doorbell and pounding on the door for a few minutes, I remembered that the Weibles had told me the week earlier they would be visiting family in Ohio over the holiday weekend, so they were not home. That was a relief.

After confirming my neighbors were not in danger, with my cordless phone in hand, made the 911 call to report my home on fire. So, now I am standing outside barefoot in my t-shirt and shorts with a cordless phone after making the call, my only possession other than the clothes on my back that I walked out of the house with, standing out in the dark early morning. I did not even have my eye glasses. My family is inside the neighbor's house with only what they woke up wearing. *"Naked I came forth from my mother's womb, and naked shall I go back again. The Lord gave and the lord has taken away; blessed be the name of the Lord."*[13] After reporting the fire to 911, I stood there looking at my cordless phone thinking how useless it was now with the rest of it back inside the burning house. I remember saying to myself with a grin, "what am I going to use this for now?" I kind of hated to throw it away, because that represented my family's only possession left other than what they all were wearing.

While in the middle of my 911 call, I heard the smoke detectors in the internal part of the house start to sound their shrill alarm. I figured that we had about 15 minutes from the time awakened by Cathy to investigate the fire odor until the fire first broke through the walls of the house. The magnitude of the timing of our wake up suddenly hit home hard. If we had been awakened by the smoke detectors going off, our home exit would have been much more traumatic and dangerous. Not being able to see into the house, it was not possible to see exactly where the fire broke through. Likely spots would have been our bedroom wall next to the attic (the door out from our room was also attached, adjacent to that same wall near the entrance upstairs to the stairway), the stair wall or both. Either of the alternatives sounded filled with peril. I was so thankful that the Lord saved the day for us. My family would have been in most certain peril. Alleluia!!!

After making the 911 call, I had a few minutes to myself to pause while standing outside waiting for the firemen to arrive. It was a strange moment, but with all the havoc going on about 20 yards away, I looked up and noticed what a glorious morning God had prepared for us. The sky was dark blue with moon and stars twinkling. It was a nice warm clear morning. As I stood in my shorts and T-shirt, the air felt like the perfect temperature – warm but not too warm; cool but not too cool. If one was to want to wake up and take a walk in the cool quiet early morning, this would be the type of morning that one would think perfect for that. I guess the tranquility of that early morning was an ironic twist to the raging fire that just drove my family and me from

---

[13] Job 1:21

our home. The tranquility of the early morning, though, was the backdrop for the tornadic storm that was the Holy Spirit heading toward us to energize and to catch my community on fire.

I now stood outside on the opposite side of the street from our burning home waiting for the fire department to come. While waiting, the fire finally became visible from the outside for the first time and I had my first look at the carnage that the fire had begun. The first thing that happened was the garage door opened by itself. Probably the garage door motor and mechanism burnt up since the fire was in the ceiling, where the garage door opener motor was mounted, eliminating the force counteracting the garage door spring. The entire contents of the garage were on fire – cars and all. It was at this point that I firmly came to the realization that my family would lose everything. The fire would not be tamed until the contents of our home were completely ravaged. The fire was an unstoppable raging avalanche that had to run its course before it would be through with us, with our home.

While watching the cars burn, I became concerned if the gas in their gas tanks would explode or not. A gas explosion would certainly add additional peril to the situation. The gas tank seals; however, just let go with an anticlimactic "shush" sound and, thank God, no explosions. It almost had the feel of a science experiment. Something that I had always wondered about and now had the answer. Seeing the two cars there caused me to realize the foolishness of persons so passionate about making sure they always are seen driving the latest, fanciest, and trendiest car. From what I saw then, it would not have mattered if the cars were Porches. They would be just as much on fire and just as worthless then to me. They would be just a metal chassis sitting in the middle of the garage and that is all they were when all was said and done.

Just before the firemen arrived, the fire broke out of the east wall of the garage. Unfortunately, the natural gas line was also mounted to the east wall of the house. The gas pipe went up the outside of the garage wall and into the house at the second floor to then run over to the laundry room, which was on the second floor, to the dryer. As the fire worsened on the east side of the house, the gas line burst and bent the pipe back 45° pointing the pipe directly toward the next door house. It resembled a large flare with flames shooting out from the end of the pipe. The most sorrowful part of the fire experience was watching the flames from the gas pipe, now flamethrower, reach our neighbors' house and ignite it on fire as well. It was bad enough watching my house burn, but seeing my friend's home burning, that was hard to take. I knew that was going to be a tough phone call to make.

The firemen arrived a few minutes later and knew they had their work cut out for them with two houses now burning. Looking now at my house, again, I had resigned the fact that it was going to be a total loss so had no grand expectations. By this time the flames were quite spectacular, especially set in contrast with the early morning dark. Both roofs of both houses were lit up in flames reaching high into the sky. Now, the only clouds in the blue sky were streams of smoke billowing from our two houses. Our house was being totally consumed and the only thing the firemen could do was to get the flames under control and out as quickly as possible from both houses, so no other families would be swallowed into the tragedy.

Now that the firemen were there and on the job, I thought, "oh good my work is done here". I walked over to the captain, introduced myself and announced if he needed anything that I would be at the Crawfords – pointing to which house that was. The captain informed me that I would be standing right there with him. If there was any emergency or information they needed to fight the fire, there would not be time to run over to find and get me out of the house. So, I had to stand across the street to watch my house burn down (and here is where the grabbing the pair of shorts came in handy – I didn't have to stand there in my underwear).

The flame's heat was intense. Even standing across the street, the heat was intense enough to make me feel uncomfortable. I felt as if I was slowly baking standing there. After the fire, one could see heat damage ripples across the plastic siding on the front of the house across the street.

While standing across the street watching the flames, it suddenly hit me! Here it is! This is the "bad thing" that Jesus was preparing me for! This is it! This is it! Suddenly, this event started to feel Old Testament Biblical. I felt like Moses (as St Pope John Paull II described earlier) at the burning bush. *"There an angel of the Lord appeared to him in fire flaming out of a bush... God said, 'Come no nearer! Remove the sandals from your feet for the place where you stand is holy ground.'"*[14] There I was, standing barefoot, watching my house ablaze. The only difference was; my house was definitely being consumed. Regardless, I had this compelling feeling that I was indeed on holy ground. My knees felt week. As before during my prayer meetings with the Lord earlier in the year, I felt the need to kneel in homage of the great power of the Lord. That; however, I did not do. I stayed planted on my feet. My whole demeanor; however, changed.

> *"'Go outside and stand on the mountain before the Lord; the Lord will be passing by.' A strong wind was rending the mountains and crushing rocks before the Lord – but the Lord was not in the wind. After the wind there was an earthquake – but the Lord was not in the earthquake. After the earthquake there was fire – but the Lord was not in the fire. After the fire there was a tiny whispering sound. When he heard this, Elijah hid his face in his cloak and went out and stood at the entrance of the cave."*[15]

Similar to Elijah, I felt the presence of the Lord, but unlike Elijah's experience, my message from God did not come from a tiny whispering sound, it came from a full out raging fire. I now knew this was the event that the Lord had foretold during my earlier prayer sessions. I felt lighter than air. I finally had the ultimate validation that those discussions with the Lord earlier in the year were in fact real. And then the realization that everything had happened just as the Lord

---

[14] Exodus 3:2 and 3:5
[15] 1 Kings 19:11-13

had promised – something bad happened and no one in the family had so much as a scratch.

The second thing that hit hard was another Biblical feeling. This time from the New Testament. This one from the Sermon on the Mount (or Plain – Matthew vs. Luke). The Beatitude, *"Blessed are you who are poor, for the kingdom of God is yours"*[16] suddenly came into clear focus to me as I was standing there gazing at the raging fire that is/was my home. Here I was. My only known possessions were the clothes on my back. I had no wallet, no shoes, no eye glasses. All the possessions I had worked to buy and amass were now inside a burning hulk of a house in process of being consumed and gone. Fortunately for Cathy and I, we weren't what you call "high maintenance", but we did accumulate things and as we found out later when going through the insurance claim process. So, on the fateful day of July 5, 1996, we had nothing - we did not even have a house and were now homeless.

To a lot of people, a riches to rags scenario would be earth shattering and totally the worst thing that could ever imaginably happen to them. With the preparation Jesus put me through, I suddenly felt the release of losing all my possessions. It was as if a weight was being removed from my shoulders. I truly had no possessions and it actually felt good, releasing, cleansing. It was at that point that I really appreciated what the Beatitudes really meant. It was not just some saying that made you feel good because you were leading a pretty good life. In Jesus' ministry, he never implied that Salvation was easy, or you just had to live a good life. His preaching was tough, gut wrenching. Just ask the Pharisees how they felt about Jesus' teaching. The fire and its aftermath were real tough lessons, *"This saying is hard; who can accept it."*[17] To truly have the Kingdom of God be ours, one has to have no attachments to their things – no other gods. One has to be prepared to lose all possessions and be joyous.

> *"Jesus said to him, 'If you wish to be perfect, go sell what you have and give to the poor and you will have*

---

[16] Luke 6:20
[17] John 6:60

> *treasure in heaven. Then come, follow me.' When the young man heard this statement, he went away sad, for he had many possessions.*"[18]

I will admit, the experience, as it was felt on that morning, was a strange feeling indeed. Something never before experienced. It probably was not since birth that I had fewer worldly possessions, but I always had a roof over my head and somewhere to come home to. That now had drastically changed in a matter of a few hours. I felt a little lost, confused, but gained a major new insight about life. I found that I was so gratified and thankful that, in spite of losing all my worldly gained possessions, I had fully intact and unharmed all the God given gifts – Cathy, Emily, Steven and Elizabeth. I had a quick epiphany that nothing else really mattered that day other than my family was safe. I found that I was prepared to lose everything if that meant keeping what God had gifted to me safely intact. This feeling of gain in the face of loss, in retrospect, was radically counter intuitive to what I and one from the world would have expected. It just goes to show that God's Spirit can do radical things within your heart if one lets Him in.

I was thankful that the Lord prepared me and did not "go away sad for I had many possessions" that day. I knew that I had my work cut out for myself. The first point of business would be to secure a roof over my family's head. All I could think, at that time, was, "It would have been nice if I had at least thought to grab my wallet when leaving." I would at least have had credit cards in hand that could be used to get our life started. This was one thing that we had to offer up to Jesus. He was definitely in control. He had His plan that we were a part of. The plan was in motion. My feeling resembled a surfer riding the wave wherever and how far it would take me and my family.

At one point soon after the firemen arrived, with both houses on fire, the fire crew had to make some tough decisions managing the resources that they had at the scene. The fire captain came over to me

---

[18] Matthew 19:21-22

and informed that they were now going to concentrate on our neighbor's home to get its fire out because there was no saving our home. That was another sobering event in the early morning's episodes, having a second person confirm what I already had resigned, that we had totally lost our home and all possessions inside. Now, fully aware that the fire was part of God's plan for our family, was OK and at peace with the captain's decision. I was glad that the fire crew was then going to try to save as much as possible for my neighbor – especially since they were totally innocent bystanders to the happening. I was also glad that the fire crew was doing everything they could to prevent further spread to other's homes as well. Two homes on fire were definitely two too many already.

Now, as the commotion, the lights from the fire trucks and roar of the fire woke up neighbors, people started to come out to see what was going on. Some were glad that it wasn't their home. Some were broken down in pure sorrow for us because they put themselves in our shoes and felt the immense loss that the fire was causing on our lovely home and possessions.

One of my most vivid memories of the fire scene was when one of our closest friends Janet Cross, that lived 3 doors away from us, came over to console me. Janet's sons and daughter were Stevens and Elizabeth's ages and were constant friends. We had many cook outs and parties together and enjoyed sitting on the driveway in our fold up chairs with a cooler of beer watching the kids in the neighborhood play a spirited game of street hockey. Janet came over to me in tears and gave me a big hug and said, "I'm soooo sorry John". I think I caught her by complete surprise when I looked at her with the biggest smile and said, "Janet, it's ok. It's only stuff." I do not believe that she believed that I was serious so came back a second time with the same condolence.

I found myself then in a conundrum. I was trying to find words how to convey such an irrational response to a most obvious situation. My response, as mentioned above, was even surprising to me. Had this same fire happened without Jesus' preparation, I am sure that I to would have been devastated by such a loss. I have seen news videos with interviews of people in our same situation after a home fire or tornado hit. Some were devastated. Others had a similar response that I gave – "the thing that matters is that we all got out ok". I remember thinking that these people were just saying that and inside had to be all torn up. They were just putting on a brave front.

The news stories that are still unfathomable to me, now more than before the fire, are the cases where a family member(s) are lost in a house fire. That, I still have no answer to how that sense of loss must feel. Now, every time I watch such a news story of a home lost, I always root for the person being interviewed – "Come on, be thankful for what you still have. Be thankful for the gift of being able to stand there alive to do the interview. It will be ok."

So, I did my best to console Janet and all the other neighbors that did the same thing that day and the days after. I am not sure if my neighbors thought I was crazy or just trying to put on the brave look. I hope I did the Lord's first teaching of the day – worldly goods are not what makes you happy and keeps your world spinning on its axis. Fulton J Sheen once said, *"You must remember to love people and use things, rather than to love things and use people."* This was the lesson that I was learning first hand and was one that the Lord had worked through me to communicate to the people that encountered our fire tragedy.

One interesting if not humorous side action during the fire happened about an hour after the fire crew arrived. The captain and I were standing next to each other watching the fire fight in progress. Now, Cathy was deathly against fireworks. Not sure where that started, but one incident when Steven was about three years old, he grabbed the wrong end of a just spent sparkler and burned his hand. I am not sure if that was the catalyst to our no fireworks at home or not, but we had not so much as a sparkler at our house. We were in a no firework zone!

Now, the berm/park, that was behind our house, had a hill at the back corner of the park near the entrance to our subdivision (Fountain Village). In the winter time, the hill was a popular place for neighborhood kids (and the adult kids alike) to go sledding on when covered with snow. Our house was one of the closest to the hill so we were hot chocolate central during sledding season.

Being the $4^{th}$ of July, the day leading up to the fire, when we arrived home after our $4^{th}$ picnic outing, there were a number of kids/people up on the hill shooting off any number of rocketing and exploding fireworks plus the typical firecracker etc. We could still hear the popping of their fireworks as we went to bed.

So, between our and the house next door, with the dark night backdrop, we started seeing firecrackers going off. They would jump up and fizz-bang go off. There had to be at least 15-20 firecrackers that were going off, one after another. The Fire Captain turned to me and asked, "Where does your family keep your fireworks?" I answered that we did not have any. He asked again, "No, we need to make sure we know where your fireworks are so my guys stay safe when they enter into your house. So where do you keep your fireworks?" He was shocked because my family must have been the only one on the planet not to have fireworks. I responded again that we had none. The Captain was not done yet. He walked over to our friend Janet and asked her the same question. She responded correctly that our family did not have fireworks. He asked several other people and not getting the answer he expected to be an obvious response, he returned back with a puzzled look and we watched the rest of the fire as the firecrackers finally ended their last.

Now it does not appear that the fireworks had anything to do with the origin of the fire, but the poor boys must have seen the smoke starting to rise from the garage and thought that possibly a stray bottle rocket of theirs must have hit the house and they were in big trouble. Possibly, in their escape, they ran between the two houses and aborted their remaining unexploded cash of firecrackers there as they ran between the houses. I am hoping they accidentally dropped their firecrackers, because if not, they put us in danger. Not because they possibly caused the fire but they saw the fire and did not do anything to wake us up and try to get us out. Fear sometimes causes one to make bad decisions. They were fortunate that the Lord was working on our side anyway that early morning.

As the sun came up and the fire died down, the total destruction and the immenseness of the loss was now totally visible and made real. The view of the burned out hulk of a house was gruesome. Our two cars, two charred metal chassis, were sitting in the middle of rubble in the garage. The roof was totally consumed and gone. The outer side walls were still there, but the top of the walls were sculpted by the burnt edges where the walls met the roof. All the windows were busted out after the firemen entered the house to put out the remaining interior fire. The neighbor's roof of their home was completely gone as well but not nearly the damage as ours, but still appeared to be a total loss on their side.

The ground surrounding our house was piled with the inside contents mainly from our upstairs rooms. The firemen tossed out anything that was smoldering, so it could be directly addressed, and they could make sure, before they left, the fire would not spark up again. It looked as if our life was spilled out on our front and back lawns. It was humbling and a feeling of being violated that our "personal contents" were now on display to all who passed by. There were mattresses, clothes, dressers, kids' toys, books etc. littering the lawn. It was as if God was saying with an exclamation point, "This stuff does not matter. It is just clutter as it now clutters your front yard!"

Then there was the smell. The odor of smoldering char. The countless things and materials that now sat wet and charred. The smell alone was humbling. It was the smell of possessions gone. It was the smell of all the attachment I had to those possessions that was keeping me away from total love of God. Blinders, they served to block my vision and my buy in to Jesus' teachings. I felt bad that my neighborhood was forced to endure this same scene of destruction until this all was cleaned up. Our home was situated near the mouth of one of the main thoroughfares in and out of our subdivision. Each morning and evening, when leaving to and returning home from work, I knew that our dismal burned out hulk of a house would be the last memory of leaving the subdivision and one of the first things seen upon returning every day when going about their daily activities. My only hope was the mess could be cleaned up soon.

Next, when the fire department cleared us to do so, we were able to go into the house and look for things that we could salvage. When we first walked in, the immenseness of the damage was breathtaking, but there were rays of wonder and excitement at the rare things that amazingly survived.

The first thing we did was to go upstairs. The stairwell was intact and safe to walk up. There were charred remnants that fell from the ceiling and covered over the stairs, but they were passable. The upstairs rooms were sobering. Each bore evidence that if our wake up sequence was delayed just a few more minutes later, some of us may not be walking through the house right then. When we walked into Emily's room, which was first room on the right from the stairs, her room was gutted. Everything that resided in her room was blackened and charred. The second sobering observation we saw, there was a large portion of the house's beam that had fallen directly across her bed. We said many prayers of thanks that Emily was not laying in her bed at the time the beam let loose! On Emily's bed we found her favorite stuffed companion, Lamby, who was still recognizable but had lost a good portion of its outer furry material. Steven and Elizabeth's room were in similar conditions - also a complete loss. Every content that once resided inside the kids' bedroom was either charred or tossed on the lawn (also pretty much charred). In Elizabeth's room we found the first survivor. She had a favorite stuffed toy that happened to be inside a charred but intact wood chest that for some reason did not get totally consumed or tossed out. When we opened the lid of the chest, there was Elizabeth's favorite cuddle toy. She walked out hugging her favorite stuffed toy as one of the few souvenirs of the day.

It was a strange sight upstairs. It was a similar sensation as being in a convertible car with the top down. We were in what used to be inside but, since the whole roof was gone, we could look right up to the sky. Next came other discoveries when we walked into Cathy and my bedroom. Our room had a desk that was butted up, centered against the attic (north) wall. There on the desk was my wallet. It was wet, smoke damaged and full of soot but still intact. The wall behind the desk was totally gone, so it was a complete surprise that the desk was even still there and not consumed along with the wall directly behind it. I would later find out that my credit cards still worked and the little bit of cash that was in the wallet was still there and definitely spendable. The rest of the room was pretty gutted.

The next discovery, which I felt was actually quite miraculous, we kept several boxes and albums of photos on the top shelf, just below the ceiling, in the master closet. Of all the things that people in our condition frequently miss the most after a house fire or tornado is the loss of family pictures, the history of one's family.

The closet was located on the west wall of our bedroom, perpendicular to the attic wall. The shelf and boxes were right there just below the ceiling. We pulled down these family treasures and they were not even wet! The roof was gone only a foot above. I do not know how many hundreds of gallons of water the firemen shot up and onto the top of the house. There should be no reason why first, the pictures were not totally burned up and secondly, what was left over should have been a puddle of mush. To have these pictures was indeed a treasure and again a miracle. Not all our pictures; however, made it. All the pictures hanging on the walls were scorched, including our wedding portraits and other family portrait pictures.

Those few things were pretty much all that was salvageable from the upstairs. We still had only the clothes on our backs. We were wearing borrowed shoes. I still did not have a pair of glasses because my original ones were gone.

So, the scavenger hunt ventured downstairs to look for any surviving possessions and mementos. The fire kicked through the wall of the garage and scorched the family room. Cathy's dad had made a nice wood shelving unit that went up both sides of the fire place then spanned across the top joining both sides. At the bottom of both side sections were storage cabinets. On top of one of the cabinets sat our TV. Inside the two cabinets below were VCR tapes which were stored below the TV and toys and games on the opposite side. Everything above the cabinets was melted, scorched or vaporized. This is the side of the house (east wall) where the gas pipe was attached to.

The next little miracle was on the TV side. The TV was melted sitting on top of the cabinet. Upon opening the cabinet doors below, the VCR tapes were intact and playable, including the one VCR tape that was the last recording of my dad two weeks before he passed away. The tape captured my dad telling one of his patented jokes where he forgot the punch line. It was those little things that put a little brightness on a day facing the look of devastation.

As we inspected toward the west side of the ground floor of the house – opposite side of the house from where the fire started. The destruction was not as bad, but everything pretty much had water or smoke damage and was not salvageable. The one possession that I was really sad to lose was a wood carved picture plaque of the Last Supper, inherited from my grandmother Chomistek after she passed away. It was always one of my favorite memories from my grandmother's house. It hung over her kitchen table and I loved to look at it. It seemed always to be welcoming me to break bread with grandma and the family. It, unfortunately was scorched black and was not salvageable.

We were able to salvage a few things, such as our good china and a few other odds and ends. In general, the place and possessions were a complete loss. One thing that amazed me about the intensity of the heat of the fire was, other than the two metal car chassis, all other contents in the garage, metal or other materials were vaporized. Gone without a trace. The one reoccurring theme that went with us throughout the house tour again was the constant stench of charred stuff. I will never forget that smell.

So, at the end of the walk through, the family walked out with a few mementos and the few things above that survived. We counted ourselves extremely blessed and fortunate after seeing the carnage done to the house, especially in the bedroom areas where we so thinly escaped. But escape we did, just as the Lord had promised.

The last downside for the day was burying our two cats who were the only living casualties of the fire. Again, they hid, and I could not find them before my hasty exit. One of the firemen, before leaving, told me where he found the bodies of the two cats and that he found the two together where they breathed their last. He had put them in a bag on the back outside porch, so the kids would not see them. I had to borrow a shovel and buried the two in what had been our family vegetable garden. The garden was noted in the neighborhood for supplying the neighborhood with bountiful amounts of Indiana tomatoes. The garden was my favorite place in the backyard so figured it was the best place to plant the two old cats. The ironic fact about our two cats, both cats were inherited from different people from different states – one from Cathy's sister living in Detroit, and the second from Cathy's best friend and fellow teacher there in Indianapolis. Both cats were completely white. One would swear that both came from the same litter.

We were pretty sure that the worst was now behind us. All we had to do now was rebuild and move on. *"Trust in Him at all times, O my people! Pour out your hearts before Him; God is our refuge."*[19] At that point, we had nothing else other than God's refuge. We were homeless and for all practical purposes, everything we owned was gone. All we had to our names were the clothes on our backs and a few odd possessions that we were fortunate to recover.

To my amazement, all the while we walked the house and saw all the destruction, I continued to have the Beatific feeling of complete poverty and a new found level of God's love and peace gained with losing the attachment of my worldly possessions, which was then accentuated by the joy that I still had all my family intact and unhurt around me. Again, that day fulfilled the Jimmy V definition of a Heck of a Day! We had a little laughter at finding the odd items salvageable. We pondered how God saved us from harm and what He then had in mind for us going forward after this new gift of life was received. Our emotions were moved to tears. And since we all survived, my family's story is still untold and unfolding as we speak.

---

[19] Psalm 62:9

## Pictures From The House After The Fire

The following pictures were taken the day after the fire (July 6, 1996). As can be seen by the pictures taken from the outside, the garage had already been boarded up prior to these pictures. Also, one vehicle frame (the Plymouth Voyager minivan) had already been towed away, leaving only the Plymouth Spirit.

View of front of home

John and Cathy's bedroom – Neighbor's home in background. Attic/garage wall was left of desk. Our bed sat to the right of the desk.

Emily's Room (next to stairs) looking out towards the north.

Stairwell looking down from 2nd floor

Family Room (Garage is the left wall of the room)

Kitchen

Kids' things tossed from upstairs rooms

One of the two burned out cars, damaged neighbor's house to left.

# I Have Come To Set The Earth On Fire

Steven's favorite cuddle toy, Squeaky

Steven (9), Emily (12), Elizabeth (7)

## Chapter 4: The Reality Sets In - Getting Life Restarted Again

With the light of that Friday morning now up, the fire out and firemen gone, reality of the situation was beginning to set in. The house, cars and all else were gone. We had a big mess to get cleaned up. The house and its contents, inside and out, were now a safety hazard. I needed to start putting the pieces back together. Our family was huddled together at the Crawford's house across the street as our new temporary home base.

That morning, we had a chance to get a few hours of sleep after the fire was out. The first two people that greeted us in the morning were the Pastor of St Lawrence Catholic Church and the Principal of St. Lawrence's school. I was surprised that word got out so quickly that they were already visiting. It was about 9:00am. Well, their visit constituted the first act of charity that we received. They came carrying a check for $500 that they withdrew from the parish's emergency fund and presented it to us. I felt so flattered that they took the time that morning to come out to console my family and me. I was overwhelmed that they would take from the church's treasure to give back to a family in need. We always think it is our duty to tithe to the Church. Here it showed that the Church in its mercy also tithes to the poor and those in need. That is one of the missions of the Church. The Church's detractors see all the money come in and all the glorious art adorning churches around the world etc. and knock the Church because of its wealth. What is not seen is how the Church, in its global mission, tithes as well right back to the world in need.

My next chore was not so wondrous. I had to contact our State Farm insurance agent to get the insurance claim process going and to find out what steps I needed to accomplish to get the house taken care of etc. My insurance adjuster gave me some names of salvage companies to start the cleanup. He also said that he would be right out with an initial check for living expenses to get us started. The adjuster gave me the name of a car rental place that would give a good deal on a car (rented older model cars).

I had to call my place of employment, Alcoa CSI, to inform them that I would have to take a few days off to get my family situated. They were very supportive and was given the time off I needed. My next tasks were to call the utility companies, newspaper, TV cable etc. to cancel services to the house. That ended a full morning of calls that no one really wants to or enjoys making.

The State Farm agent as promised promptly arrived with check in hand. That was good to see and the second real bit of good news of the day. We had funds (about $1500 if I remember) to start the recovery process. It looked as if the process was going to go smoothly from that point on.

So, in the afternoon, I picked up the rental car, which was a 1990 Chevy Impala, and then we had wheels. I made reservations at a nearby hotel for a few days, so we had at least a place to sleep that night. The next day, we received a call from a friend, Maria Shipley, who our kids went to St Lawrence Elementary school together, who had just earned her realtor's license. She indicated she would help us find a longer term temporary housing option. Angels, such as Maria, were constantly put in our service by the Lord and this theme goes on as God's plan now unfolds.

The next several days, we slept at the hotel then came back to the Crawford's house to set up home base for each day's efforts of recovery. The day after the fire, July 6th, the company selected to clean up the debris, arrived and started removing the rubble around the house. I was so glad to see them come because I was really worried that some curious kid or treasure hunter would injure themselves trying to enter and walk through the premises. That is when the second round of fireworks started to happen.

As I mentioned earlier, my next-door neighbor's house was also seriously damaged. So now we had two damaged houses with two insurance claims at two different insurance companies. When the insurance agent for our next-door neighbor saw the cleanup in progress, he went ballistic. Contrary to other trains of thought, insurance companies are not in the business of just handing out checks.

Even though we pay our hefty monthly insurance premiums, Insurance companies will find every chance they get to find someone or some company at fault to file law suits(s) to recover some or all of their insurance disbursement. The other insurance agent was now charging State Farm with tampering with evidence. They wanted to investigate the fire to find someone/thing to sue.

My State Farm agent called to discuss the matter. He said that according to the filing done by the other insurance agent, we had to halt the cleanup effort. The only thing that we were legally allowed to do was put up a fence around the perimeter of the house to secure it until the other insurance company cleared the property for demolition. I was hoping, at least for my neighbors' sake, they would not have to put up with this still odorous eyesore for very long, and for a quick end to the investigation. Well, as everything else in this story, God's time is not as quick as mine. We finally received the ok to remove and demolish the house at the end of October. The poor neighborhood had to put up with this eyesore for almost four months.

**The Counting Of Possessions Lost**

Now the next order of business was to make a list of things that were consumed in the fire other than the cars, which fell under the auto policy. We had a $40,000 limit to personal property recovery. At the time in 1996, I thought that the total of the possessions we owned and lost would be considerably under that. I did not believe that we had amassed even anywhere near $40,000 worth of stuff. One recommendation that the insurance industry makes, and is a good one, make a video of all the contents residing in each room to provide a concrete record of what was lost. Well, we did not do that.

The process used to catalog the possessions lost was to mentally walk in and explore each room with my mind's eye, remembering the room's layout and what was positioned where. I made a list of what I saw in each room. As my mind's eye walked into each room, the list grew, and grew, and grew. By the time done, I was shocked to see that we had amassed even considerably more than $40,000 worth of possessions. In fact, I had a nice chunk over and above the $40,000 to deduct from my income taxes that year for the "loss" deduction.

This exercise really opened my eyes as to how many possessions we really had. Newton's law of universal gravitation states: *"Any two bodies in the universe attract each other with a force that is directly proportional to the product of their masses and inversely proportional to the square of the distance between them."*[20] If we look at the size of our attachment to our possessions as an opposing mass to attract our love, or allegiance away from God and His love and mercy, even if we had just a little attachment to each of those items (we had to have had some attachment or we would not have gone through the trouble to keep them in the first place), when all the little attachments and the bigger attachments are added up, how massive would our possession gravitational attraction be? How far did the force of those attachments make me drift from my love of God? How much did I love my stuff vs. the love I could have had for God?

This exercise brought out two thoughts posed from the massive list of lost possessions. First, it confirmed my feeling of freedom from my possessions lost, of total poverty; the feeling of a deeper inheritance of the Kingdom of God as it states in the Beatitudes. On the other hand, it gave me pause to ponder the future. I knew that this feeling of total poverty and homelessness was a temporary phenomenon. One that I would always remember and cherish in my heart, but knowing, with insurance money coming my way, soon I would be buying back things, rebuilding our home and we would be back owning possessions again. I hoped what my family would take from this experience going forward was to first be a better steward of our possessions - remember the poor - and not to get caught up needing and buying things just to have stuff around. Also, to at least assign an even smaller level of attachment to the things we did have, thus giving a stronger attachment and love of Christ.

---

[20] Wikipedia, Newton's Law of universal gravitation

## Lawyers – Who Needs Lawyers?

The day of the fire we talked to Cathy's brother Larry, who was a lawyer in Detroit. I wanted to get a feeling from him to confirm that I was performing all the right steps to work the insurance and any other legal matters that Cathy and I should be attending to. The first words out of his mouth were, "Get a lawyer!" I thanked him for his advice and talked it over with Cathy. We decided that the insurance company was being more than fair to us so far, so we thought we could handle it. Those prophetic words from the brother in law were to ring true in a short time.

A short while later, I started getting calls from State Farm interviewing me with questions about the fire to take general information of what happened. This at first caught me a little off guard, but knowing that there was the other insurance company involved, I, at that time, saw State Farm as putting together evidence and a story that would protect us from any legal action that this other insurance company may take against us.

This questioning process went on for several rounds. The questions were fairly similar each time, so I was easily able to give factual and honest responses and no warning signals were going off. Then one of these interview sessions took a new and ominous turn. The questions started as normal asking for scene of the fire type questions. Then a different tone started. "You have a 9-year-old son correct?" I answered yes. "Can you tell me what he was doing that night?" and went on to ask if Steven was playing with fireworks that evening. Well, the warning whistles started blowing hard. My instant thought – "Time to get a lawyer!!"

This was no easy task for us. We had never professionally talked to or sought out a lawyer's services before. Just the fact that a prior trusted ally, our insurance company, had just turned on us was frightening. Now we had to find someone in the law profession that we could trust our livelihood with. Well, as it turned out, the Lord put a really good lawyer right in our back pocket. One of our parishioners at St Lawrence, who also was on the CRHP presenting team for my initial CRHP retreat, was a lawyer. In fact, he once even worked for

# I Have Come To Set The Earth On Fire

State Farm and knew them well. Initially I wasn't sure how fond of Kevin I was. He was always an opinionated and in your face kind of guy – a lawyer – and that tended to rub me the wrong way a bit at times. Once we began to discuss our situation with Kevin, we knew he was our lawyer. He was a deeply religious and orthodox Catholic. He knew and seemed to have an ax to grind with State Farm and he was a pit bull on the loose.

It took almost a year to totally settle our claim. Kevin even made several trips to State Farm's headquarters in Illinois to meet with upper executives. He was able to make sure first that we received all the insurance adjustment payments that were due to us, made sure we stayed out of any law suits and made sure that State Farm did not drop us or raise our insurance rates.

There were other Godly given coincidences that happened through Kevin's leadership on our case that worked to better our leverage with the two insurance companies. Late in August, the two insurance agencies were still squabbling over what caused the fire and who was to blame. Still at that time no one had been able to determine the actual cause of the blaze. It so happened that a prominent forensic fire accident investigator was in town for some professional function who was an acquaintance of Kevin. Two weeks after our fire TWA flight 800 left from JFK airport and exploded in midair just as it cleared the Long Island coast into the Atlantic killing all 230 people aboard. One of the theories explained the explosion to be caused from the impact and explosion of a missile shot from some unknown location – so the investigation was front page news for weeks. The forensic investigator secured by Kevin was one of the prominent investigators hired by the FAA to investigate the crash and just happened to be visiting Indianapolis. He was able to look over the fire scene and assigned the cause as electrical in nature. Although not able to exactly pinpoint the precise origin, he did rule out a number of theories of what the fire origin could have been (e.g. fireworks). What he did provide was the evidence needed to at least exonerate our family from the origin of the cause discussion brewing between the two insurance companies. We then received a free pass from litigation, which was comforting, considering the tone the insurance company investigations had taken to date. God came through for us again, and again in a mysterious/miraculous fashion.

**Temporary Housing**

The first piece of business for the family was to find a place to stay. We stayed three days at the hotel. God stepped in again for us. One of our good friends in the neighborhood was going on vacation that next week, so Monday (July 8) we took residence at the Peterson's home. Our next challenge, find a temporary apartment or something to move into by the end of that week before the Petersons returned home.

Our realtor friend Maria Shipley had just started work at a realty company called Tucker. She took us on as a mission to find our new temporary home that we could rent until the house was rebuilt. Maria donated her time all that week to ferry us around the Castleton and Geist areas looking at rental properties. We finally found a lovely condo that was right on a little inlet bay on Geist Reservoir. The family that owned the condo had moved out and bought another home. The price was right and could not beat the view. I guess it was another gift from God for the cross that He thrust on us to bear to fulfill His plan. Also, for all the work Maria did to help us find the condo, she refused take a dime for her effort.

I wanted to take this time to send blessings to the Shipley family. In the several years after the fire, the Lord dealt the Shipley family some mammoth sized crosses to bear themselves. Maria's husband Ed was diagnosed with brain cancer. He survived after several surgeries and chemo regimens, but finally passed away. That was not bad enough, but about five years after that, Maria was killed in a motorcycle accident. In a short number of years, the four children from the Shipley family (who were about the age of our kids at that time) tragically lost both mother and father. God bless the souls of Maria and Ed. May they bask forever in the Lord's greatness and love. And also God bless Maria and Ed's children. May the blessed spirit of their mother and father burn bright and the Christ like example they exhibited to the world burn bright in their memory. May they emulate

Maria and Ed's example of how to live a holy and loving Christ filled life.

We enjoyed living at the condo. We lived there for about six months. The only thing that I felt bad about was, we were not with the old neighborhood. The neighbors in our subdivision had to put up with the burned out hulk of a house every day and we were snug in our new condo on the lake. I knew that our neighbors would eventually have hard feelings towards us as they thought we were now out of sight and out of mind. I could not blame anyone that came to that conclusion, but Cathy and I were doing all we could, within the confines of the two insurance companies, to attain approval to remove the dwelling and rebuild.

It felt strange residing in the new condo. Being temporary, it was hard to feel at home there. Everything felt different, not ours. It was a lot smaller than the house. Even our furniture was temporary – rented. So there was a lot of adjusting to do. The kids did enjoy feeding the ducks and playing with a family of feral cats that visited us frequently. Even with the nice condo setting, I longed to get this temporary situation over with and get more permanence back in our lives.

**Tear Down That House!**

As time went on and the insurance companies continued to squabble to assign blame for the house fire, days turned into weeks and weeks turned into months and the burned out house stayed up. The other insurance company allowed us to at least clean up the lawn, but everything in the house and garage stayed as it was the day of the fire. The only thing we were allowed to do was to maintain the fence erected around the house to prevent people from entering the premises and injuring themselves. So again, the house was at the mouth of the main in and out street to and through the neighborhood. For almost four months, all neighbors that left the neighborhood to go to work or other places had to pass by this huge eyesore. And it did not smell very well either. There was a nice play park right next door on the west side of our property with a swing and other play equipment. Families of course were now hesitant to come with their kids to the park, which was too bad. It was always one of the neighborhood's gathering places.

Neighborhood sentiment started to sour as the weeks and months went on, and again, I could not blame them one bit. I tried to keep the home owner's association up to speed with what was going on with the insurance side. They kept asking when we would tear down the house. I was frustrated because I had no answer. The only thing I could say was the demolition of the house had to wait until the OK from both insurance companies was received. I knew there would be hard feelings since we had moved out from the neighborhood, thinking we were abandoning them or were not putting forth our best effort to expedite the home demolition because we were out of sight and out of mind. There was no way I could convey my feelings of anguish felt because of the eyesore the neighborhood was forced to suffer through and to put up with.

In early October, we were served a complaint document from the Department of Health and Safety that one or more residents had filed complaining the house was unsafe and a health hazard. For a brief moment I had a feeling of disappointment that one of my neighbors would write me up especially since the reason that hulk of a house was still standing up was really the fault of the insurance companies and not mine. I quickly came to my senses and confirmed that if I were in this person's shoes, I would have done exactly the same thing. In fact, I was surprised it took that long.

The complaint seemed to have made a dent in the insurance companies' priorities. It took about another two weeks, but finally the long awaited call from my lawyer was finally received. We were cleared to tear the house down. It was the week of Halloween that we finally demolished the house. That was a good day. It felt comparable to former President Reagan's – *"Mr. Gorbachev, tear down that wall!"*[21] And the walls did come down and the rebuilding started. We

---

[21] Speech given by President Regan at the Brandenburg Gate, Germany June 12, 1987

could see the light at the end of the tunnel now. The race was almost over.

The next decision we had to make was whether the family would move into the rebuilt home or would we sell the new home and purchase another. We debated our course of action and prayed over it. In the end we made the decision to sell the rebuilt home after it was completed and buy another house. We were concerned that the kids were too traumatized having to flee the house and would have bad feelings and dreams if moved back into the house after rebuilt.

So our St. Maria gathered us up again and we started looking for our next house. By the grace of God, our finances were better than I expected. We did well thanks to Kevin and our insurance claims, and people were also generous to us as I will discuss later. We found that we could afford to buy a house even before we sold the one we were rebuilding. Maria again donated her time to drive us around looking at properties. We ended up buying a house in the Geist Reservoir area that was considerably bigger than the last one. It was a beautiful house. We had great neighbors that we are still friends with. And Maria donated her commission back to us to help buy down the house cost.

I never thought that we could afford to live in the Geist area. It was one of the affluent areas of Indianapolis. For instance, the Indiana Pacers' best player at the time, Reggie Miller, lived on the pricy side of the reservoir. His home was not too far away from our temporary condo and that Halloween our kids were fortunate enough to trick-o-treat at his house. There were homes worth well over $1 million in the area but there were also pockets of homes that were a bit more reasonable, and we got a good deal on our home price as well. I always joked that our new house was a partial lake view property because in the winter, when all the trees lost their leaves, if you looked real hard out the back door, you could see some water in the far distance.

So, we moved into this big house, but we really did not have anything to put in it, considering all our home furnishings from the prior house were consumed in the fire. When we moved into the small condo, the only things we actually purchased and owned were our beds. All other furniture was rented and returned when we moved from the condo. We had not received our total insurance compensation, so could not afford to go out and buy all new furniture, especially to fill this bigger floor plan. So, for the next several months, our house was full of empty rooms. Our family room, for instance, was a "bring your own chair" only area. The kids loved it because the empty room made for a large indoor playroom with plenty of running room. Moving into the new house and living in a bare home was another example where things, once taken for granted, now felt as if there was a void in our house and lifestyle – something felt missing. It was also a continuing reminder of the level of possessions we once accumulated. We got by fine without all the furniture. It probably looked a little strange, I am sure to our neighbors, when they came over to visit, as they probably had the same sort of feeling, "There is something missing here?"

**You Have Got To Be Kidding!**

About the end of August, we were settling up with the auto insurance to complete our insurance settlement on the two cars. That was the only insurance exercise that actually went smoothly. So, on this date, we were attending our final appointment with the adjustor at the State Farm office. Everything was going well. Papers were being drawn and signed. We were in our final discussions and instructions about what was to happen next to get our check.

I do not remember what the issue was, but Cathy started to question something. It started as a normal discussion would. Then her voice spiraled up to this whiney hormonal tone and she broke out in tears as she was talking. I had heard that tone before – three times before. All I could think of was, "Boy are you pregnant! Lord what are you doing to us now?"

After our meeting was over, I had a little talk with Cathy and I told her about my observation that she was pregnant, and she should set up a doctor visit to check it out. She disagreed with my assessment but set up the appointment anyway. And, I was right. We had number 4 on the way. At first, I saw the event as another cross that the Lord had hung Cathy and me on. In my thinking, with all that we had going on at that time, a baby was the last thing we needed. Besides Cathy was approaching 40 at the time and we had read articles about the higher birth problem risks associated for mothers 40 and older. I quickly realized that the baby was not just a gift by the Lord, but the most precious gift he could have given us. God really took care of us and we definitely profited much more than we lost due to the fire. I was going to be a dad again!

It was a great experience, though, buying the replacement cars. First, I was so glad to finally be in a position to return back the old rental clunker that we had been driving. I felt like a big shot, waltzing into the auto show rooms. The salesman would walk up and ask what kind of car we were interested to look at. We promptly answered, "Yes, but we are actually looking to buy two cars, and we will be paying cash for both as well." That usually commanded an increased level of respect. One could see the $$$ signs light up in the salesman's eyes.

We finally settled to buy two Plymouths – a $10^{th}$ anniversary special promotion package Voyager mini-van (with options that we never dreamed of) and a Breeze. The Plymouth dealer we bought the cars from gave us a great deal. First, Cathy's dad was a foreman at Chrysler, so we were eligible for the Chrysler employee family discount. On top of that, the dealer was in the process to move the dealership to a new location, so he gave us an additional moving discount on top of that. We were back to a two car family again.

**Do You Still Love Me?**

In John 21:15-17, Jesus asks Peter three times if he loves Him. Peter answers with increasing concern why Jesus repeats the question, after Peter repeatedly answers "Yes". I had a similar experience later that same year.

I worked for a company called Alcoa CSI. Alcoa, of course, is a large producer of aluminum products, but the CSI stood for Closure Systems International. Although CSI originally manufactured and sold aluminum roll-on closures, now the large majority of the caps sold were plastic. I worked as a Systems Engineer in their

Sales/Customer Service Team group. One project that I was working on involved launching a new injection molded cap which was being developed and molded at a 3rd party injection molding company located in Elgin, IL. After living for two years in Streamwood, IL, which was about ten miles away from Elgin, we learned not to refer to Elgin as a suburb of Chicago. Streamwood was a suburb; Elgin was not. The people would curtly correct you if you made the cardinal error. So as you can surmise, if you were not familiar with where Elgin is, it was a similar drive time as traveling to Chicago, which took about three hours from Indianapolis.

The meeting was scheduled for Monday morning and I had to meet another engineer from the Alcoa Crawfordsville plant in Elgin at 9:00am. I left the condo at about 5:00am for the trip up. Most of the trip was spent driving on interstate I-65 which spans from Indianapolis up to the northwestern corner of Indiana.

The morning was a nice crisp November morning. The weather was fine; it was just early. As I entered onto the interstate, I said a Rosary for safe travel and a successful meeting. Traffic was light due to the early morning time of the day but there were a few cars that I could see in the distance in front of me and also in my rear view mirror. It was still dark, but the eastern horizon was starting to lighten for the days coming sunlight.

I had finished my Rosary a few minutes before as I was now cruising northbound along Interstate 65. Then things started to get a little more exciting. A southbound trucker fell asleep at his wheel. I saw the truck up ahead on the southbound side of the interstate start to veer off the road and hit the middle berm separating the north and south lanes. He took a 90° turn through the median and was heading straight for me. There were instantly a hundred thoughts going through my head. Everything seemed to be going in slow motion. It seemed that any evasive action taken would not be productive. No matter what I did – speed up, slow down – it looked as if the truck had me dead to rights either way. I remember thinking to the Lord, "Is this how it is going to end after all we went through this summer?" So, I decided my best recourse was to try to keep my car under the best control possible and move over as far as I could and hope that the driver, as he bounced through the median, would wake up and take the proper evasive action to miss me.

I am not sure if the Lord was trying to ask me that third time for me to confirm my love for Him. Possibly the Lord has a warped sense of humor – just kidding. Since I am writing this, it is pretty obvious that I survived. The driver in fact did wake up and as soon as he cleared the grass onto my side of the interstate, he cranked his wheel and was able to get his truck turned now heading south on the northbound interstate lanes, missing me by a few feet. That was enough to get my heart pounding for the rest of the day for sure. No coffee needed.

After that happened, I remained in a state of concern because now we had a semi-trailer truck heading south on the northbound lanes and as I mentioned earlier, there were cars maybe not even a quarter of a mile behind. I watched in my rear view mirror and saw cars veering wildly and the truck finally turning back into the median, coming to a stop. Thankfully, there were no accidents that happened during this event. All that remained were stories to be told of how all survived the wrong way semi-truck.

I eventually arrived at the molder's plant and waited for the person from Crawfordsville that I was to meet up with. He arrived about a half hour after I did. He had to take the same interstate route that I did so when he arrived, he promptly excitedly asked, "Did you see that big semi in the median on I-65?" "Yes", I said to him. "That semi and I got up close and personal with each other." I told him the rest of story.

For a second time in a matter of a few months, the Lord had pulled me out of a potentially deadly situation, completely unscathed. I am yet to figure out the reason for this second episode, but undoubtedly it was part of God's plan in some way. Maybe I was starting to forget the Spiritual experience from the fire and started to sway back to "the real world". Perhaps God needed me to hang in there a bit more to complete His total plan. God, I really do love You!!!

## Chapter 5: The Face Of Angels

Now comes my favorite chapter of the book. In the aftermath of the fire that first morning, I was sure that there would be more of a role that the Lord had in mind for me. He went to elaborate lengths to prepare me for something. The fire was definitely one of those somethings. I had to wait to see what else God had in mind.

The first of that "something" happened during the fire and immediately afterwards. Our neighbors took us in. We were want for nothing. We had places to stay, food to eat, drink to drink. We had lunch and dinner at a different neighbor's house each day. Cathy and I joked that we were scouting for the future family we wanted to eventually move in with who had the best tasting meals. Our friends showed their unconditional love and care to help us begin to put the pieces back together.

And then the real "show" started. God's plan began to take shape – at least as it was revealed to me. Beginning with the morning visit from our pastor, Fr. Mark Svarczkopf, and school principal, Sr. Mary O'Brien, from St. Lawrence, the various communities we touched and were a part of started to show up, over the next two weeks, in a steady stream of Good Samaritans. I was totally taken back. Not in my wildest dreams did I expect such a loving turnout of people that wanted to help us.

This perplexed me because I had never been in this situation before. America is such an affluent country and one full of charity. During charity situations I had been involved in in the past, I was usually on the giving side of the picture. Now being so needy after the fire, it put me in a unique position of being the subject of charity. What should my reaction be? There are all these people coming to give me clothes, food, money and other things for the family. Should I be gracious, sad, happy? I definitely wanted to convey that we were so appreciative of all their generosity, but I had never had to do this on such a grand scale before and did not want the people to go away with any less feeling than of our total gratitude. So, I did my best.

But come they did. Person after person started showing up at the doorstep of our neighbor's home, where we stayed, with gifts of all sorts of necessities that we needed to get on with life. People brought clothes – shirts, pants, shoes - for the kids, Cathy and me (some did not exactly fit but when you do not have any to start with, we were more than happy to wear them just the same). People brought bedding, dishes, silverware, and cups. People brought baseball bats, ball gloves, soccer balls, dolls, books and other toys and stuffed animals for the kids. Every day, someone showed up with either a lunch or dinner precooked and ready to eat for us. Of course, a number of the people donated money as well. People also gave us general wishes that if we needed anything, just call. The best thing was, they really meant it. Their "just call" wish was not just a "box checking" comment, hoping that we would not take them up on it. It was a genuine gift of continuing service as needed. All were deeply cherished and especially, on those first days after the fire when we were in such dire need for everything and anything, were so vital for our family.

It was amazing the number of things that we used every day and blindly relied on their presence and availability throughout our day, that we never gave a second thought about until that first day when all were gone. It was those every day, taken for granted things that we were most gratified to receive from our benefactors. Our entire daily routine was now altered because our time, space and environment we lived in was now changed, different. We now lacked the basic building components of our daily lives. We now had to work around to negotiate these holes in our normal daily functions.

Basic staples like toiletries, clothes, shoes, a house with its utility functions – shower, cooking, laundry etc. - were no longer in our possession and control. To gain those and other daily supplies and services, we had to resort to ask others to borrow or obtain the supply. This endeavor puts one in an extremely humbling condition, when I cannot even produce the simplest of living supplies for family and me as I once did without any difficulty.

This was new ground for sure for the whole family. I can never think of a time or day when I was concerned where I would sleep or how I would feed my family. I never had a second thought that I did not have another set of clothes to change into when I woke up the next morning. I never contemplated that I would be in a situation where I needed someone to give me a pair of shoes because I did not have one. Receiving these things was humbling for sure, but it really drove home the realization of all the "mundane, every day" gifts that God had put into our lives that we really failed to notice or even see them as gifts because of their everyday familiar nature - we had seriously taken them for granted.

All these acts of kindness and generosity gave my family some hope and a window to see that we were, and we were going to be all right. We could see that God was taking care of us. We were not orphaned or cut off from our community by being driven out of our home. We found that the house is not your place marker to define and keep you in a community. Community is not a grouping of houses. Community is a grouping of people. Our communities made sure that we knew that we were still welcome and valued members. Our community surrounded us, pulled us up from the abyss, put us on their backs and put us on a level footing where we could resume our lives productively again. That is what a Christian community does and how one works!

As people visited to drop off their assistance to us, I began to experience a multitude of feelings and emotions. First, as stated above was the humbling reality that I was poor, in need for the first time in my life, and these people were drawn here to provide me aide. At first, I did not relish the fact that I was poor. One of my initial feelings in this vein of thought was, by being poor, the persons with means were above me. I felt like I was looking up at them as if they were somehow better, higher in standing than I was; that I had less worth because I was now poor. I felt a sense of embarrassment that these people had to go out of their way and take time from their valuable days to pick my poor behind up off the mat because I was not capable to do so.

But I began to notice that the people that came to visit looked different. Some I knew well. Some I saw only at church or other activities. With this diverse grouping, demographic of people that came out to our aid, there was something that seemed to be in common with each one. There seemed to be a common denominator present. They were not inconvenienced at all. The people who came to offer their charity to my family seemed to have a glow about them. It was Jesus!

Ever since grade school at Blessed Sacrament in Midland, MI, I had been taught that Jesus resided in every person's heart. I always believed that to be true, at least as a point of Faith, but until that day of July 5th, I never really understood what that statement really meant. Of the many gifts that I received over the year of 1996, the vision of Jesus in each person, was one of the most jaw dropping revelations in my life. I believe what the Lord showed me, was a little of His vantage point towards how He sees His beloved creation. He showed me the jaw dropping beauty, the agape love, the goodness packed within each I encountered.

Now, I am not sure that I can fully describe the vision of Jesus that each person exhibited. Their smile was wider, gentler and genuine. Their eyes twinkled and were bright and wide in delight. The people, as they visited, resembled the description of the Three Magi as they reverently came bearing and presenting their gifts that first Christmas. These people's chests were pumped out in joy – in a humble way. When they exited, I am not sure if their feet touched the ground because their demeanor was so light, Spirit filled and full of energy. Person after person visited to provide their gift. The look on their faces was angelic. I could see how filled with the Holy Spirit they were. It was as if their charity balloon had been blowing up and blowing up, expanding and expanding. It was being held back by something. Then the house fire and BOOM their charity burst wide open. The pent up charity and God's love suddenly burst from their bodies and out their faces. They could not help but pass on their charity. My family was the fortunate conduit to their release of charity.

It was as if they were sent to share much more than just the gift that was brought. My friends (new and old) were there to share a piece of themselves as well. They were there to share the Jesus in their hearts. I could see the Jesus level build in their hearts from the moment they pulled up to the curb until the time they left. They truly walked away radiating with 100 times more Jesus in their hearts than they had upon the start of their day. I could see then, how wonderful they felt. It appeared to be one of those types of situations resembling one's going to Confession. You wait. You have excuses why you do not go. Then you finally go and receive forgiveness for your sins. It feels so wonderful that you think to yourself, "Why did I wait so long? This is so wonderful!" I am sure that the people that came out those days and weeks after the fire wish they could bottle up that joy to have forever.

My role in God's plan became somewhat clear from that point on. God had used my family's fire tragedy to energize His people in and around the Castleton and Lawrence Townships, and St. Lawrence parish areas. I found myself in a wonderful position. I felt like I was in the stands watching an outdoor Shakespearean play unfolding in front of my eyes. Once I figured out that through our tragedy, God had energized the groups and peoples around me, it was a glorious thing to watch unfold. I saw ordinary people turn into saints and angels. I got to see the face of Jesus every day in every person who visited. Now that was a heck of a week. That was something special.

**Family to The Rescue**

It is in real times of need when one finds out where their friends and family really stand. Our family did not hesitate once the news about the fire was received. For instance, Cathy's sisters showed up within 24 hours, both Geri who lived in Detroit and the youngest sister Michelle in Cincinnati. They came out with the main goal to love and support us.

After they arrived that day, Geri and Michelle took a tour through the house with us on the day after the fire and helped us celebrate that we were all still on this earth and lived to tell about it. Geri also was our photographer. She took pictures of the house, inside and out. At first it felt a little strange to capture the destructed property remains. It felt akin to photographing a wake or funeral. But the photos, such as those included in this book, were the product of Geri's photo journalism and are now cherished heirlooms, chronicling the day that God changed our world in a few short hours. The photos were also valued evidence used by our lawyer to chronicle the site of the fire for later use. The photos she took preserved the memory of a dark morning that the sun did finally come up. The memory that God's will was done. My family can point to those pictures to celebrate that He loved us enough to spare us from real danger when imminent danger was all around.

Being there, I believe, helped Geri and Michelle console and love us – just what we needed. Having a chance to walk through the burnt remains gave them a sense of what their sister's family had just survived. It gave them an appreciation of the trauma that we had just been through. It also provided the vision of how destitute my family was; that we had no possessions and that meeting our base needs would be a powerful means to accomplish their goal of support.

One of the works that Cathy's sisters undertook to achieve was somehow finding ways to provide means of linking us back to the family's state of equilibrium enjoyed in life prior to the fire. The first attempt was to replace things like favorite toys or stuffed animals for the kids. One of these favorite toys, Emily's favorite stuffed companion, Lamby, survived the fire, but had "3$^{rd}$ degree burns" over about half of his body – outer material was singed away. Geri and Michelle decided to go out and find another Lamby II to replace Emily's original best buddy. I was deeply impressed. Lamby was light blue and had a wind up music box in its stomach. They actually found a dark blue Lamby, even with the same music box, that was identical except for the color. When brought back, it was nice, but Emily did not immediately warm up to it. Lamby II was not the same.

To add the final touch, Geri performed surgery and replaced the burnt parts of the original Lamby by cutting away the dark blue fur/fabric from the dark blue lamb and sewed that to replace the burned and missing fur on the real Lamby. Emily, now married and with our first grandchild, still has that stuffed toy Lamby laying on her bed today. That present was so special to Emily, getting her stuffed friend back. It did not matter that Lamby now had dark blue splotches. She had her special friend back, something that then linked her to a less complex time before the fire.

The one thing that really hit me when observing Geri and Michelle those few days spent with us was the joy that they had in their eyes. It was the same Christ like smile and beaming aura that I saw from the other people that visited as they delivered their charitable contributions. They knew they were doing a work of mercy and their faces also beamed as if they were angels.

These are the sort of things that our family did for us. The common denominator in all what our family did again was the look (and sound when done at long distance phone) of joy. Joy at being able to aid a family member in need. Joy that my family was alive and well which was something to celebrate!

Cathy and I knew that we would not get everything back that was lost – nor did we really want to replace all because we had more than we needed. Our family did the best they could to comfort and help get our lives back on our feet – because that is what family does. I am sure the fire period was probably a worse experience for our families than it was for us.

After all, I think my sisters in law kind of enjoyed flirting with the hunky firemen, as they came back to check on the house, anyway. I think we received a few extra visits by the firemen as well – just to make certain the fire did not come back to life I am sure.

## Volunteer Groups Come To Our Aid

As mentioned earlier in this story, both Cathy and I were involved in a number of volunteer, work, school, church and other organizations. The shocking thing that totally caught me off guard was each of the groups, that Cathy and I were some part of, came to our aid. The working of the Holy Spirit was not just relegated to St. Lawrence parishioners, nor were Catholics the only recipients.

The first thing that blew me away was that people would actually go out of their way to visit. That was one of my most cherished memories. At the time of the fire, GPS and Garmin units were not commercially available yet so our visitors had to do some work to find us. It was not the money or items donated that was so special, it was the fact that these people went out of their way to first find out where we lived, where we were staying, make a special trip to visit, then provide whatever support they could. I am sure each of these Good Samaritans had plenty of other important and fun things to do that day. But these people, that day, made the commitment to forgo those important/fun things to do something even more important and glorious; something commanded by Jesus - make that special trip to visit and help their neighbor out in whatever way they could. It does not get any better than that.

The second thing that blew me away was the wide array of people that visited. We had people from the school that Cathy taught in Warren Township visit. We had people that had girls in my wife's Girl Scout troop that she led visit. Men and women from the St Lawrence CRHP program came out (Cathy also attended a women's CRHP). Families from the Cub Scouts that I was an assistant Den leader came out. My fellow workers at Alcoa pitched in and gave me money to buy my three kids new bikes.

I think the group that floored me the most was the soccer league that my kids played in and I coached in's outpouring of support. Representatives from the Lawrence recreational soccer league showed up with a gift certificate from the local soccer store to buy my three kids new soccer equipment. That meant that the soccer store also was touched by this Holy Spirit filled tidal wave. The charity of a secular sports league we participated in caught me totally unawares. I was so totally filled with gratitude for this and all the selfless acts of charity that we were given by our communities.

Next it was amazing to watch our various groups spring into action to plan and execute fundraisers on our behalf. The first one was put together by the Cub Scouts. The Cub Den was made up of St.

Lawrence 3rd graders. They then conspired with their parents to hold a car wash fund raiser for us. The fundraiser was held at the St. Lawrence church parking lot. The day of the car wash, I took Steven, who was my Cub Scout, and we went over to check out how the car wash was going. We pulled up and parked on the opposite side of the parking lot. I stopped, and we got out there because I did not want to interrupt the angelic atmosphere I saw going on. It was a great thing to watch. Again, the look on each of the car washer's face was so beautiful. I pointed that out to Steven. I said, "Look at their faces. Have you seen anything so beautiful as that?" Again, it was as if we were watching a great movie. It felt surreal. The scene was so glorious it almost did not look earthly. And it probably was not. They were angels in action. The amount of money they raised was deeply appreciated, but paled in comparison to how much I enjoyed watching God's love in action, transforming normal boys and their dads into saints and angels.

Another surprise happened when the St. Lawrence Parish took up a second collection at Mass two weeks after the fire specifically for us. The showing of community charity made me feel so special. My Church was collecting money for my family! That was a very moving experience. Again, the amount of money collected and provided was a blessed gift, but the real gift was just the sharing of love that my fellow parishioners exhibited to our family.

My family was at church that Sunday, and first, it felt strange watching the basket being passed through the congregation knowing it was for our benefit. I felt bad not contributing anything as the basket passed our way. But I was amazed that almost everyone was dropping some contribution into the basket as it passed. This was for us! People that only knew us as a parish family in need were gladly opening up their wallets to contribute to a fellow parishioner that had fallen on hard times. That is what a Church does! *"All who believed were together and had all things in common; they would sell their property and possessions and divide them among all according to each one's need."[22]*

I was so moved by this demonstration of Church community and the numbers of individual parishioners that went out of their way to visit and offer help, that I asked Fr. Mark if at the next Sunday Mass, I could address the parish to show my gratitude for all that was done for my family. He agreed. That next Sunday, I stood at the pulpit and thanked the St. Lawrence faithful. That talk was one of the more moving things that I have done to date in my life; to stand at the pulpit and humbly acknowledge the generosity and kindness of my fellow parishioners. That is what a Christian community is and does.

A third event held on our behalf was a cookout carnival benefit put together by my subdivision. People in our subdivision decorated and set up the play park, which was next door to our home. The Homeowner's Association then put together a cookout and sold hot dogs and hamburgers. They also had games set up for the kids. All done to raise funds to donate to my family. They even arranged for one of the TV stations in Indianapolis to come out and cover the carnival. At one point, with the burned out home in the background, Cathy and I were interviewed of which I again pledged my heart felt appreciation for all the support and love given by our communities and especially our neighborhood. As mentioned earlier, I am not sure that my neighbors would have had the same festive charitable feelings after a month or two with the house remaining a constant eye sore. At least, in the end, I was gladly able to donate the money they raised back to the Homeowner's Association as a show of gratitude to the neighbors that had to put up with the charred house for so long.

It was quite apparent, after all was said and done, that the little that Cathy and I had achieved by volunteering and be involved in our individual groups we participated in, had been paid back in more than full. In the Old Testament Book of Job, it says, *"The Lord restored the prosperity of Job, after he prayed for his friends; the Lord even gave*

---

[22] Acts 2:44-45

*Job twice as much as he had before."*[23] I felt the same way. We received so much more than we gave.

In the end, the lasting impression I will always have from the fire episode was the radiant faces from each of the people that came to our aid, from Geri and Michelle to the scouts at the car wash. Their angelic look melted my heart with God's mercy shining through. To actually have seen Jesus shining in and out from each person was so special. It was as if I was seated in the balcony suite for a grand opera which played out right in front of me, watching God's plan unfold. It was as if I was the only one that had the play bill. Seeing a Spirit invigorated community is something to behold! If the whole world ran that way I think the Garden of Eden would be put to shame.

**The Final Gift**

The final gift that we received arrived nine months and two weeks after the fire. Ryan Joseph's birth was our final gift. We called him our little fire baby or bonus. Ryan was a bonus for the whole family. All our other children were significantly older. Liz our previous youngest was almost nine when Ryan was born. Emily, our oldest was 13. Ryan was like their little baby doll. It was great! We had built in babysitters.

Steven was excited as well. Cathy kept calling Steven "our next little Priest". Steve then felt that he was off the hook because now Ryan could hold that honor. Steve, I hate to bust your bubble, but I am still praying for that Priesthood for you. Just wanted to let you know.

Ryan completed our family. He is now an Eagle Scout. Graduated High School with a 4.12 grade point average and is now a freshman computer science major at Texas A&M University – our third Aggie – where he just completed his first year's studies with a 4.0 average as well.

Again, my first impression when Cathy was initially confirmed pregnant was of concern about added complexity that a 4$^{th}$, and a baby

---

[23] Job 42:10

as well, would add to our family. All the other kids were now in school, which meant we no longer had to be concerned with daycare arrangements for the first time in 13 years. Sometimes it takes a while for God's gifts to really sink in. Sometimes God's gifts do not look or feel like a gift, or anything that we actually asked for, at first receipt. Ryan was just as precious as any of the other three. God knew exactly the gift we lacked, we needed – number four.

Here stands the next challenge. Throughout the years leading up to the fire, I was adding to my "works" bank account. I know I had to have some "good works" deposited in my account but one can never be sure how much is in there. After the fire, I was suddenly overdrawn - that I am sure of. The sudden outpouring or withdrawal of charity from my works bank account, after the fire, suddenly left my account overdrawn. This then meant my bank account was empty and needed to be replenished again. I was already deep in debt to the Lord for his extreme kindness and generosity, and now had an even deeper hole in my works bank account to fill.

Now, I do not want my Protestant brothers to go off on the "Saved by Faith only" tangent and how one cannot buy one's salvation – a la the works bank account. That is not what the Church teaches nor what I mean. Doing works is the bare minimum that Jesus expected and mandated in His teachings. Works flow from one's Faith. Jesus did works did He not? These works have to be the loving and selfless variety – per the mandate to love one's neighbor. Works not done for <u>my</u> benefit or edification in any way but only for God's glory. Those done for pure love of my neighbor in need.

> *"The one who had received five talents came forward bringing the additional five. He said, 'Master, you gave me five talents. See, I have made five more.' His master said to him, 'Well done, my good and faithful servant. Since you were faithful in small matters, I*

> *will give you great responsibilities. Come, share your master's joy."*[24]

This passage from Matthew shows that we must always strive to use our gifts given by God every day to glorify Him; to be the angel that others were to me during our fire experience. If we are not diligently working to do God's will that fills one's works bank account, we are then just as the servant burying one's gifts in the ground. We are being the equivalent of a "Christian couch potato". We are not or even refusing to do God's will.

So, now the big challenge, to get that works bank account full. Not by doing random things just to say I am filling my account. *"When you give alms, do not blow a trumpet before you, as the hypocrites do in the synagogues and in the streets to win the praise of others. Amen, I say to you, they have received their reward."*[25] The works I am talking about are ones done out of love and because Jesus expects and commands me to do them. They are works that Jesus is asking me to confirm my "Yes" to His will and plan for Salvation. Those are the ones that fill up my works bank account. So I can "come and share my Master's joy".

> *I pray that all my readers will share in our Master's joy by saying "Yes" to Jesus when called to do His will to be part of His Prayer for the Salvation of humanity. Amen*

---

[24] Matthew 25:20-21
[25] Matthew 6:2

I Have Come To Set The Earth On Fire

# Part 2: Takeaways From The Fire Experience

The important part of this story is not the fire itself or how much we as a family lost in the fire. The fire scene represented the starting line, the launching pad for the rest of the story. The important things to take from the fire story are: what was learned by the experience and how people were affected (both short and long term) do to all's involvement and proximity to the event as it unfolded. If nothing was indeed learned or benefited from the fire experience, then what happened was a true tragedy. That was not the case by any stretch of the imagination.

It is amazing how one event can touch so many teaching elements and emotions that my family and I will remember and take with us for the rest of our lives. The following chapters dive deeper into these individual lessons learned to provide a more in depth view of the power of God that was on display and the greatness and infinite love and mercy shown as well. These chapters are not to be thought of as an exclusive list of what was learned for there was much more.

Chapters in Part 2

Chapter 6: Humility Hurts

Chapter 7: Why Do Bad Things Happen to Good People?

Chapter 8: Power Of Prayer

Chapter 9: God Given Gifts vs. Own Earned Wealth

Chapter 10: We Take A Lot Of Things For Granted

Chapter 11: The Essence Of True Peace

Chapter 12: Paid Back In Full

Chapter 13: Doing God's Will Breads Disciples

Chapter 14: New Appreciation Of The Beatitudes

Chapter 15: Go Tell It On The Mountain!

Chapter 16: God's Most Precious Gift – My Family

## Chapter 6: Humility Hurts

I could go on for pages chronicling every act of kindness and charity that we received but these acts of charity caused another emotion to kick in; another gift of God given to me from the fire experience. I would like to start this section with a question. What does "Humility" really mean? We have a number of words that have several levels of meaning or action. For instance: capital "**C**" Church stands for the entire universal Catholic Church. Small letter "**c**" church stands for the church building that you attend Mass at daily or weekly. Another good example in the Church is capital "**T**" Tradition vs. small "**t**" tradition where Tradition is the teaching of the Apostles handed down through the Church not positively chronicled in the Bible but in union with it. Where traditions in the Church are long standing practices that were added throughout the centuries of the Church that are not binding on Church teaching but good things to do to bring us closer to God.

Now humility is another such word that I learned through my fire journey that has the same multiple levels of feeling. The sensation of small "**h**" **h**umility I have found to resemble a whittling of a stick with a pocket knife. Those life situations only shave into the first layer of humility/ego. Situations where one has been publicly scolded or "dressed down" by another person may cause embarrassment; one to ponder whether the act done was right, wrong, or was only a dressing down embarrassment caused by a person just having a bad day. One experiencing this level of humility may feel a little **h**umbled by the situation, but the humility does not cut deep. We get over it!

The fire event was the first event I had experienced that cut deep into my psyche, into my pride. A capital "**H**" Humbling situation is not a whittled shave but a deep saw cut. One that cuts deep down into the marrow. A full **H**umbling experience causes one to deeply ponder about the relationship one has with his Creator, his Lord and Savior. One realizes an imbalance in his/her life from the one that God has given him/her. To resolve a full **H**umbling type problem, one must take that situation to God in prayer. One needs to make things right by God to continue on one's journey toward salvation.

Of all the occasions of charity that my family and I experienced during the fire journey, there is one that stands out that put me into a Humbling situation. One day when the family was at the Crawford's house about one week after the fire, a lady that I knew from church pulled up and parked in front of the Crawford's house. Now, when I say I knew her from church. I had seen her every Sunday. We both routinely went to the same Mass time. She and her family always sat on the opposite side of church from us, so I did not really know her, I just recognized her. I did not even know her name.

She walked up to the house and I met her at the front porch. Pointing across the street to what was left of our home, asked if I was the one from the house fire. I acknowledged that to be true. She reached into her purse, pulled out her checkbook and asked, *"Who do I make this check to?"* Now, she by far was not the first person to donate something to us, but for some reason having some semi-stranger write me a check right in front of me really cut deep into my humility and pride. It almost felt like a dagger in the stomach. No offense meant to the writer of the check. It was me. My ego was suddenly tweaked. Again, I was accustomed to be the person "writing the check" and my ego took a big bruising.

There were only a few seconds between when the question was asked and my final response, maybe only three to five seconds. But these five seconds seemed to have dragged on for hours as I pondered the question. The problem was, there was a big battle waging in my gut. A battle waging between my ego vs. what I needed to do to fulfill God's plan for me. There was a layer of ego fat that coated my heart and what this lady was asking me to do was cutting deep into that ego fat layer.

Perhaps, since this was later in the week after the fire, I had seen my share of charity given for the week already. I do not know. Charity is sometimes difficult to be on the receiving end of. It forces you to come to grips within your psyche that "Yes, I am needy. I am in need of my neighbor's and God's mercy and charity." For some reason, I guess, I did not really see myself as "needy" in prior occasions where people stopped by to donate. For some reason, God picked this woman and her charity to force this bit of reality to hit home. At that very moment, I saw my own personal spiritual vulnerability as if I were peering at myself through my soul's mirror. This event had exposed my ego to its core. It put me on dangerous ground where I may choose for myself, to appease my ego, and choose against God.

I paused for a second and said a little prayer to God asking, "What do You want me to do?" My first inclination that my ego was telling me to do was, "Decline the check because she at that time probably needed the money more than I did." Actually, the real reason I wanted to decline her check was that her writing me a check had tweaked my ego and that made me feel uncomfortable.

My response back from God was quick and clear. This scene playing out was not about me getting money from her. It was all about her writing the check and giving it to me. It was about her mercy being energized. So again my "would be" prideful reaction was not what was in God's will. Had I declined the check as I wanted to, I would have worked against God's plan. *"Peter took Him aside and began to rebuke him, 'God forbid, Lord! No such thing shall ever happen to you.' He turned to Peter, 'Get behind Me Satan! You are an obstacle to me. You are thinking not as God does, but as human beings do.'"*[26] As happened to Peter, Jesus took exception to Peter's attempt at derailing God's will and plan. He would have taken exception to me as well if I had refused the check, because my initial inclination to decline the check was thinking as a prideful human does, not as God wished me to act.

I gave the lady my name. I watched as she filled out the check and as usual, had to help her spell my last name. I am not sure which was more difficult, the whole day of July 5 or this one short five-minute visit to accept a check from a fellow parishioner that I did not even personally know.

I think the reason this episode was so impactful was, she was not a personal acquaintance. It was easier to accept help from people that I

---

[26] Matthew 16:22-23

knew. *"And if you greet your brothers only, what is unusual about that? Do not the pagans do the same?"*[27] Again, help from friends is a normal occurrence. It happens all the time, although not on the magnitude of what was experienced after the fire. I help friends in need and they help me when I am in need. This was different. This lady was not one in my inner circle of friends nor one that I could even recite her name.

In the end I felt good. My ego was a bit bruised, but I was sure that I did the right and good thing. I would recover. I was sure, though, that I played another part of God's plan to energize His people. This may sound weird, but I did the charitable thing by accepting the lady's charity.

> *I pray that we all listen to and take to heart God's call when a humbling situation happens; taking the time to truly learn and benefit from the problem felt; using the lessons learned to become closer to God and His path for us to our Salvation. Amen.*

---

[27] Matthew 5:47

## Chapter 7: Why Do Bad Things Happen To Good People?

> *"My son, when you come to serve the Lord, prepare yourself for trials. Be sincere of heart and steadfast, undisturbed in time of adversity. Cling to him, forsake him not; thus will your future be great. Accept whatever befalls you, in crushing misfortune be patient; for in fire gold is tested, and worthy men in the crucible of humiliation. Trust God and he will help you; make straight your ways and hope in him.*
>
> *"You who fear the Lord, wait for his mercy, turn not away lest you fail. You who fear the Lord, trust him, and your reward will not be lost. You who fear the Lord, hope for good things, for lasting joy and mercy."* [28]

Why really bad things happen to good people has been questioned and a source of confusion since man first set foot on this planet - since the first mastodon fell on top of the village chief. Throughout the Old Testament, and common sentiment even through to today, holds if one does well in the eyes of God, He will bless you. That has been mistakenly interpreted to mean that a good person deserves a peaceful, undisturbed life and unmeasurable wealth. A good person was synonymous with wealth even back in the Old Testament. Look at how the Old Testament passages describe the patriarch's "Favor" with God, e.g. Abraham and David. The passages equate the amount of God's Favor with the size of their herds, possessions and land owned.

When something bad happened to a good person during an Old Testament story, the community around this person would inevitably assume that the person or person's family (parents, grandparents…) had done something wrong, lost Favor with God, that they were being punished or cursed by God.

---

[28] Sirach 2:1-9

To date, this sediment still is alive and well. Bad things should not happen to good people. When it does, this usually shakes the psyche of world.

Another big question that has been prominent especially ever since Abraham walked the earth is, "If there is a God, why does He allow bad things to happen?" "Does he not love us?" Why would a loving father not eradicate suffering from us all and make this whole world a big Kumbaya party? *"What father among you would hand his son a snake when he asks for a fish?"*[29]

So why did a bad thing happen to, at least I think so, a good family such as ours? Since my family was subjected to this fire tragedy, was my family being singled out and punished or received some harsh sentence for some bad thing that I or someone in our family had done? Had we lost Favor with God? Perhaps we were too lukewarm in our Faith and God wanted to send a message for me to "heat" things up a bit? At least I would believe the lukewarm option as at least a partial potential motivation, but I would be totally naive and self-centered if I believed that the fire episode was totally something designed by God directed exclusively towards and for me. The obvious answer to this riddle is, the major emphasis from the story was not associated with any all-inclusive purgative nature nor to exclusively single out my family and me. In reality the fire was put into play to energize the good (not a punishment), to let loose the charity and love of one neighbor for another that was locked in place in the hearts of both my family and the surrounding people of the area.

My family played a small but vital role in a much larger plan that God had put into place to revitalize our community. A plan that involved and touched hundreds of people. God's plan did involve energizing my family and me, but, I would say, the main emphasis from this episode was actually put into play to energize the immediate world around us.

---

[29] Luke 11:11

I was able then to see two answers to the questions of why bad things happen to good people and also why God allows bad things to happen in this world.

First: Adversity makes one stronger, stronger in Faith and love of the Lord. How many times in the Bible are there references of being tested thus being strengthened? References such as gold tested and purified by fire[30]. The refiner's fire.[31]

Second: One's adversity not only makes one stronger and better, it also brings out the best in those around that person. Case in point, all the people whose charity and love burst from their souls to come to our aid. They became better persons because of our adversity and their response to that adversity.

In summary, adversity makes me a better and stronger person, friend, father and Christian. One's adversity also helps make the world a better and a Godlier place as well. The causal effect of God's total plan to raise a small, insignificant individual such as myself, served to make a significant and beneficial change registered at least by my local community. With a little ripple effect, plus the effects from other separate, parallel events that God puts into play, the worldly effect could be much larger than I can ever imagine.

Fulton Sheen once said, *"Unless there is a Good Friday in your life, there can be no Easter Sunday."* Jesus' Good Friday and Easter Sunday changed the world. When you look at my fire story, Fulton Sheen's analogy could be demonstrated in that experience as well.

- I had the Agony in the Garden when Jesus revealed to me that something bad was to happen to my family.

- The fire was my Good Friday – losing all my possessions. At least from the Apostles and Disciples point of reference that Good Friday day, they as well thought they had lost everything they expected to gain from Jesus' ministry after

---

[30] 1 Corinthians 3:12-13
[31] Malachi 3:3

- experiencing Jesus' horrible and humiliating death on the cross, just as my family and I had lost everything we thought we had in the fire.

- The revelation that the fire was the "bad thing to happen", as predicted earlier in the year, was my Resurrection day. After our resurrection day, the people that were touched around me, as well as myself included, were galvanized into a full acting Christian community. The Apostles and Disciples, that great day, knew something great happened in Jesus' rising but also knew that God's plan was still unfolding. They at that time did not have a clue as to what would happen and their role in it. I felt the same. I knew God had gone to great lengths to prepare me, as he did the Apostles, and was joyous, but I had no clue as to the greatness of God's glory that was just about to unfold and my role in that event.

So, it is put into place by God. If we are not challenged, we become soft. We do not become the best we can be without being tested. We tend, as Adam and Eve in the Genesis Garden of Eden story[32], to get complacent in our Faith and walk away from God. Salvation is not gained by comfort and contentment. What would the world look like if the world was in total peace with no evil, no bad things happening to anyone, no challenges to our Faith and way of life? Would we not have a world full of lukewarm Christians? Would we still be Christians? How could we gain Heaven in those conditions? We need adversity. We cannot gain our Heavenly rewards without adversity. Thank God that He loves us so much to have established humanity so that we can use adversity to be the basis of our "Yes" to Jesus. Thank God that He gave us a means to be passionate about our Faith and passionate about our "Yes" to serve Jesus and reap the rewards that He has promised if we follow Him. In Matthew, Jesus said, *"Whoever does not take up his cross and follow after me is not worthy of me."*[33] Our tests and adversity allows us to distinguish our

---

[32] Genesis 3
[33] Matthew 10:38

love for Jesus – do we love him a little bit, not at all or do we love Jesus with all our heart, mind and soul.

We cannot forget, as Matthew Kelly states in his book, *"Rediscovering Jesus"* that, similar to the Israelites wandering in the desert during the Exodus, searching for their "Promised Land", we are likewise all pilgrims on a journey to find Jesus; to gain our salvation. When we become comfortable, we tend to end our journey right then and there and build our walls on the spot. By truncating our journey, we fall short of Spiritual greatness that God has planned for us; fall short of our overall final rewords He has mapped out for our salvation. Thank God that Jesus loves us so infinitely to challenge us to say "Yes" to accept Him as our God and Savior.

**Be Patient, God's Work Is At Hand**

We today are so reliant on immediate gratification or immediate understanding of a situation. We ask a question and expect a prompt response. People of today, observing our gutted home back then, would only tend to see the immediate pictures of the fire tragedy – the burned out hulk of a house, the loss of all our possessions - and draw their snap conclusions that this event was nothing but a large tragedy – both in the amount lost and the fact that it happened to a good family.

In God's time; however, the answers to the question of, why God allowed a bad thing such as our fire to happen, may take years to totally play out. Over time, looking back, the picture becomes clearer and less fixated on the initial tragedy scene. If one just had a little more vision; had a little more patience to watch God's plan unfold, the picture received would be a much more complete and glorious vision. The hand of God is not the tragedy; it is the salvation that comes after adversity, which may take a while to totally play out per God's overall intentions, especially when one looks at the enormity of the overall playing field. There were hundreds of people touched in some way that came into contact in some manner with the workings of the fire scenario. It will take time for all these individual experiences to come to full fruition and radiate out.

When I say touched, I mean seeds planted. Some of the seeds sprouted immediately, thus the immediate rush of charitable responses we received. Some of the seeds may take a while to germinate, bear fruit and will sink in later on to provide the revitalized experience for the individual(s) involved. In all, the situation was quite divinely spectacular in its total effect on the people we touched through our fire ministry. The number of people, groups and organizations with seeds planted from the fire story continues to grow as my story has been spread to other communities (e.g. Our Lady of Angels in Allen, TX) and now through this book. Again, it is quite possible that the real person intended to be evangelized by this story is not born yet. *"One sows and another reaps."*[34]

As chronicled in my story thus far, it has been shown how the people surrounding us had been rejuvenated and empowered by our tragic situation. The fire was not for me and my family's benefits alone. God affected our entire community, from people we interacted with on a regular and personal level to the people that remotely touched our lives. Now I have no idea as to what total good this did for all these people involved in our story. I do not know if this burst of God's mercy and love was a onetime explosion that died out shortly after, or if lives were permanently changed because of it. That is for God to know. I believe though, my Faith tells me that yes, in some way at some level, lives were touched and changed. What a wonderful thought and memory to have, that God used His humble servant to touch and maybe save lives.

Let me throw out another theory and example to illustrate how God's love and will sometimes evolves over an extended period of time to achieve His goals. Seeing how my fire experience had longer term ramifications, I thus see similar patterns when reading the "Historic Books"[35] of the Old Testament Bible, that maps out and sets the ground floor for God's long range plan to launch His religion and

---

[34] John 4:37
[35] Joshua, Judges, Ruth, 1&2 Samuel, 1&2 Kings, 1&2 Chronicles, Ezra, Nehemiah, Tobit, Judith, Ester, and 1&2 Maccabees.

Church worldwide. When reading the Old Testament, there are a plethora of stories where bad things happen to the Israelites – God's Chosen People. The subsequent verses describe the immediate situations as seen by the eyes of person(s) in the middle of the tragedy, or at least through the lenses of the author of that book. The verbiage continually asks, "Why did this happen to us?" There is also usually a question relating to, "I thought we were Your Chosen People, why are You making us suffer?" Thirdly, there is the sediment that the happening was a response from God for some ill done – Favor lost - usually because the people fell away from worshiping Yahweh. During these periods, especially after Solomon's rule, there was the break up, separating the Israelites in the north from the Judeans to the south. Israel and Judah were then conquered, and people dragged off to foreign lands. There were subsequent persecutions driving the inhabitants to flee to other lands as well.

Now looking back from a 21st century vantage point, one can now see that the misfortunes spelled out in these Old Testament stories were much more than just punishment for sins committed. These misfortunes and disasters to the Jewish people served multiple purposes. Surely one of those purposes was to cleanse and keep the Jewish people faithful to Yahweh. Yet there was another, grander and farther reaching plan that these events came to play as God put His plans into action. They were the launching pad for Jesus' Church. The people of that day and even the Old Testament authors did not have this vantage point to look back at the whole story. What was sown by the Old Testament Jewish people's hardships was reaped by the early Christian Church centuries later.

To demonstrate, let us look at what happened when the Old Testament Jews were persecuted by the Babylonians, Persians, Greeks and Romans. Jews were now banished and dispersed all around the Mediterranean and northern African lands. Small Jewish settlements formed as little outposts.

Now after Jesus died, resurrected and subsequently formed his Church, as seen in the Book of Acts, the Church was commissioned to spread out to the whole world. Right after the Church was first formed, there was another persecution from the Jews against the Christians living in and around Jerusalem. *"On that day, there broke out a severe persecution of the church in Jerusalem, and all were scattered throughout the countryside of Judea and Samaria, except the Apostles"*[36]. So now Christians were dispersed, and where did they run to? They settled in places where there was a Jewish settlement already present. Another verse from Acts, *"Now those who had been scattered by the persecution that arose because of Stephen went as far as Phoenicia, Cyprus, and Antioch, preaching the word to no one but Jews."*[37] One can now start to see the plan unfold.

When Paul set out on his ministry mission to evangelize the known world, he followed the same pattern. He did not randomly pick the places that he chose to create Churches. He found settlements of first Jewish Christians, then other Jews. These communities were already aware of Jesus or at least aware of the Salvific Old Testament Biblical promises and prophecies of the Savior to come which Jesus then fulfilled. It was to the people in these towns that Paul set out to preach about Jesus's life, death and resurrection. Cities such as Philippi, Athens, Corinth, Phoenicia, Antioch, Ephesus etc. all had Christian and/or Jewish communities. And these people were put in place initially by the Old Testament hardships causing Jewish migrations to happen. Jesus needed fertile ground for his Church to take root and flourish if it was truly to become a global Church. If only the Judeans and Israelites had been a part of the revelation of God's plan to birth His Church, those Old Testament stories, I am sure, would have a different, more hopeful tone.

The example of the epic transformation from the Old Testament history of God's People of Israel to the worldwide explosion of Jesus' Church demonstrates the length that God takes to fulfill His plans. Could God have created his Church right with Abraham? Yes, He could have. God; however, allowed His Church to evolve over many centuries to best establish it as the World's Religion. God knows us, knows His creation so well that He provided the proper environment

---

[36] Acts 8:1
[37] Acts 11:19

at the proper time for his Church to be given to us. God took tens of centuries to prepare and position His people to fulfill that part of His plan for the salvation of humanity.

God's plan did not end with the creation of His Church. That is why each one of us still gets individual callings, large or small, to further His plan. We individually feel that our tiny parts cannot amount to anything being so small in the grand scheme things – a mustard seed. When bad things happen to us, the total effect on God's plan plays an even greater role to spread salvation. A good thing does act to spread God's love. A bad thing, such as happened during our fire story, makes an even larger impression on the world; a Spiritual wake up call. The more compelling the bad thing or tragedy, the wider the net that is cast on those touched by the situation, then touched by the Holy Spirit to enter into the song.

Again, do not despair. One's adversity does not go unrewarded and does fit in God's puzzle for His overall plan. As the single note in a Mozart symphony is struck, it is difficult for that note to see that it is part of a great symphony. If that single note was left unplayed when performing the symphony, the music would be missing something, not as good or complete; with a slight hole in it. Also, the note does not know if it is at the beginning or at the end of the song. Just as when we are called to do God's will, we do not know how long it will take to play the rest of the song to reach the final climax of the performance. Nor do we know if we are part of a short musical jingle or a major opera performance. Our note is played then taken over by subsequent notes. All we can do is to have faith that in the end, God, the infinite audience, will be standing and applauding all the notes played for such a beautiful and wondrous performance completed.

So, the story goes on and on. The fire happened. I will not, until I am blessed to meet my Maker, ever know the total expanse to the good that happened; the total effect what God's actions performed through my family will have had on this world. With the initial adversity my family invested into God's plan, God kept his word and provided immensely more blessings and grace to us than we ever had before. I personally learned countless lessons about God's infinite love, humility and the challenge ahead to attain Salvation. I also was given just a little glimpse of how God's glorious will was designed to energize and invigorate the area's population, which was so beautiful and magnificent to watch. It was so enlightening to watch how God took what seemed to be an awful tragedy to turn it into a glorious celebration of His love. As happened to the Judeans of old, I was only given just a small slice of vision to God's plan, just a small little glimmer of His overall wonderful plan for humanity. It is up to the rest of the notes now to take over and be played. Glory be to God!

> *I pray that when times of trouble befall you, that you take heart that you have played possibly the most beautiful note in God's musical score of salvation, not only your salvation but the world's salvation as well. May the Lord's peace and love travel with you always in your good times, bad times, and your really bad times. Amen*

## Chapter 8: Power Of Prayer

I learned a lot about prayer over the course of the several years beginning with the CRHP experience through and after the fire experience.

    1. Prayer is always good. No matter where one is in one's Spiritual journey, prayer is essential. A personal relationship with God is vitally necessary to keep one on the route to Salvation. Even when it seems that God is not listening, He is, so keep on praying.

    2. There are definitely levels of prayer. Prayer level, I believe, has a lot to do with where one is Spiritually at the moment. During the fire sequence of my life, I was so Spiritually stoked that I saw my prayers changed. I prayed differently. My prayers became more vibrant and intense. I truly believed that God was capable and loved me enough to answer my prayers, and He did.

So, now that I am some 20 years removed from the fire, I find myself looking at my prayer life and see that there was maybe a two-year period where the Lord totally enveloped my essence. Where I was able to converse with the Lord. I felt his presence. During the winter prayer sessions, I described earlier, I actually felt as if there was something, some being in the room with me. I remember feeling a movement in the room and looking over in that direction and not seeing anything, but I felt a presence of something. Maybe it was an angel – my guardian angel perhaps. I definitely was not alone in that quiet room sitting on my Lay-Z-Boy chair reading my CRHP homework.

The feeling that I had in prayer over that period, whether I was at Mass or sitting in my Lay-Z-Boy, was indescribably wonderful. To be truly close to God felt so soothing, so enlightening, so peaceful. Prayer turned me into a bowl of Jell-O. When one totally puts him/herself in the hands of God to dialogue and most of all listen, the whole world looks in a different way.

The most vivid prayer that I encountered was a contemplative type prayer. I would be praying my word prayers and petitions to God and it was as if God told me, *"all right it is My turn to talk and you listen"*. When I totally shut down my distractions to completely block out everything except concentrating on God's message to me, the fireworks started to happen. I have mentioned several times about out of body experiences and seeming to levitate above to watch a Spiritual event unfold. Well, these contemplative prayer sessions were similar to that. I was not really aware of my surroundings at all. It seemed that I was in some 4th dimension, and that was the God dimension. I would not say that I had any sort of Heaven vision experience as one hears from people describing a return from a near death situation. It was an experience of closeness and oneness with God. As if I had God all to myself.

Did I hear any specific words? No it was not comparable to any human conversation that you and I would have. I did not hear any words but God was conveying messages to me. One might call it telepathic communication. I prefer to call it Godepathic communication. The feelings and messages that God gave me were definitely confirmed when the fire hit so I am assured that I was not making all these encounters up. At these times of prayer, when God was conveying His messages, there was never a doubt in my mind that the messages were in fact real. The only thing that He did not convey was the exact event and time. God is the prototypical Parent – need to know only. I was 100% sure that God had a plan and that I would be a part of that plan He was preparing me for. I knew it had to be big because God went through extreme means to groom me and seemed to be singling me out for some reason to be His conduit.

My whole prayer life seemed on fire. As said earlier, I prayed differently. Instead of starting my petitions with, *"Please Lord, can You..."* I always started my prayers with a much humbler, *"If it is in Your will..."* The main change to my prayer life, though, I actually believed that Jesus was hearing my prayers. I believed that Jesus was participating in my prayers. I was actually a part of my prayers. I believed that Jesus would answer my prayers. My prayers were not a "let's throw that out and see if it happens" as my prayers were before. I truly believed and felt that I was in a personal audience and relationship with the Lord. *"Prayer is not asking. Prayer is putting oneself in the hands of God, at His disposition, and listening to His voice in the depth of our hearts."*[38] I believed that my prayers were personally heard and would be acted on within the will of God for He knows best what is best for me and for humanity.

There were also monumentally answered prayers granted during this period. Some bordered on miraculous. Here are two examples.

During my CRHP formation program, a son of one of our CRHP brothers was diagnosed with a brain tumor. The son was scheduled for surgery to remove it. One evening when the CRHP group was assembled, he announced to the group about his son's tumor prognosis and about the upcoming surgery. One can imagine the deep anguish in this poor man's heart with the deep uncertainty about the welfare of his son in the ballast. We prayed over him for the success of his son's operation.

Nowadays, brain surgery is perhaps more common as surgical technology and techniques have improved. I do not care what you say, any time that a surgeon has to operate on one's brain it just seems like a miracle that God guides the surgeon's hand to remove and fix all in there without the slightest flinch that could pose disaster.

The surgery went well. The tumor was successfully removed. I remember the meeting when the dad brought the news of his son's surgery success to the group. Even though there were at least a dozen others that prayed over him that meeting before and countless others praying as well, I felt a personal tie that the Lord had answered my personal prayer. I also remember several months later when the same CRHP brother complained to us that his son had just been given a speeding ticket. I saw the same looks in most of the other guys' eyes – how great it was to even be talking about a speeding ticket when this boy was so close to not being with us.

---

[38] Mother Teresa

## I Have Come To Set The Earth On Fire

The second situation was also very similar to this one above. I had the privilege to receive another chance to sit on a CRHP formation team the following year. This CRHP formation team was too small and needed another person to have a sufficient number of members to put on the following retreat. This second CRHP retreat presentation marked the first time I was fortunate to give this fire story.

One of my fellow team members, after arriving to that evening's formation team meeting, mentioned that his daughter (a young mother) was diagnosed with cancer. Of course, he was deeply distressed and not knowing where to turn. I asked the man if we could pray over him for his daughter's health. Remembering the result in the case of the boy with the brain tumor, with this, now, being the second similar cancer patient prayer situation, I had the same Faith the Lord would hear our plea for this fellow CRHP brother.

He consented, kneeled down and we prayed over him. This time there was only four of us. Again, I am sure there were plenty of others praying in the background as well. The next week he came back with a smile on his face. We asked him how his daughter was. He said she had gone to another doctor for a second opinion and that doctor could not find any evidence of any cancer. Now one could easily argue that there was no cancer to start with and that the original doctor was mistaken in his diagnosis. We will never know the answer to that challenge one way or another again until we all meet our Maker, God willing. But doctors earn their money being very good at diagnosing illnesses and would not put one through the trauma of a potential death row sentence diagnosis if the initial doctor was not pretty sure in the first place. My feeling that I had, upon hearing the daughter was free from cancer, was one of elation! I was positive that God again had heard and responded to our prayers. He had come to our aid. I again could feel a strong link from my prayer to the definitive and glorious answer given by God to this now joyous father.

The prayers made during this time, especially when praying for the two cancer patients, contained four basic elements:

Element 1: A statement of humility, that I am not worthy and do not deserve what I am about to ask.

Element 2: A statement of Thy will and Thy will only be done. God is not a genie to grant wishes.

Element 3: The specific petition being prayed for.

Element 4: A request that the person be granted the grace and strength to persevere whatever the Lord's will is for them.

Here is an example:

> *"Lord, I know you do not owe me anything and in fact I am eternally and totally indebted to you for all I have and all I am. If it is in Your will, please…If this is not in your will, please give the patient and family the strength and peace to persevere, to carry out Your will."*

This prayer format is not to be seen as some guaranteed prayer to cure illness, but just an example of a humbler prayer form used compared to my typical pre-CRHP prayer of before that jumped right into the "*Lord could you please…*"

Regardless of the words spoken, the key to these statements of Faith is to truly believe them – mustard seed believing. If you do not believe that God is capable or loves you enough to grant your petition, your Faith will not move mountains and cure cancer. Even with a heartfelt and sincere prayer, the petition made may not be in line with God's plans. That is why it is always a good idea to add into the prayer a petition for the patience and strength for the prayer recipient(s) to accept whatever God has in mind for them. He may have had other plans for these cancer patients. God may have wanted to inspire someone with the patient's suffering faith, or the family of the cancer patient to inspire someone with their strength and faith over the ordeal.

A third thing that I became keenly aware of is that every minute of every day is a prayer to God. Every breath I take; every movement I make is a prayer to God. The way I live my life, the things I do and not do, and even my short comings can also be a prayer to God. God is watching and loving us every moment of the day so every action we do becomes a prayer back to God. My daily challenge to myself is now, how can I pray better to God today than I did yesterday? How can I bring God better into my life at each moment? How can I thank God for every breath, every step and every thought that I think and take? How can I thank him for the beauty of the world He created and gave to us to enjoy: the beautiful sunrises and sunsets, the clouds, the stars, the rain that makes things grow and green, and on and on?

By the end of that first year after the fire, the one thing that I was certain – there is a God. I talked to him personally. I saw His will carried out through my family. I personally saw the power of His will through interceding prayers by His children. Every once in a while, in a weaker moment, someone might say something that would cause me to pause and ponder the existence of God. But, I perk right up and say, *"Hey, wait a minute. I know there is a God because I talked to him, remember?"* Thanks be to God!

Now 20 years later, I long to have that same essence of closeness to God. The ability to truly have a personal conversation with Him. To feel His personal presence. To feel His power in my life as it was 20 years ago. It seems now I have distractions again, that have returned, that I did not have back then. To get back to the prayer level during the fire sequence, I will need to rid myself of these worldly distractions. Jesus made Peter, James and John come down from the mountain after the Transfiguration even though the three wanted to stay up and bask in the glory of the Lord up on top of the mountain. Jesus had other things that they were needed for, such as spreading His Word and Church to all nations. I guess I had to come down off my mountain as well and live back in the world. Like Peter, James and John, I feel my work is far from over – whatever that may be. Besides I have a whole good works bank account to fill yet.

Even so, God still talks to me. I am sure he talks to you as well, but one needs to recognize God in those calls when they happen. Did you ever have one of those sensations when perhaps at work you were looking for a solution to a problem and the solution stumped you? You racked your brains out and nothing. Finally, maybe driving to work, there is an epiphany. The solution just seems to have come out of thin air into your mind. Now some may attribute the discovery as a sign of their intelligence that they were able to figure the situation out. I hate to bust their bubble on this one. It was God who gave that epiphany gift. So, when something such as that happens, make sure to say a quick thank you prayer to our Lord for solving the problem for you.

How about a situation where you have a tough or what you perceive as a controversial discussion to be had with another person? You are agonizing leading up to the meeting concerned that the person may respond poorly at the news or discussion. But, when you actually confront this person, low and behold, everything goes great and the person actually thanks you for bringing up the topic. Again, thank you Lord for giving me a wonderful gift.

This sort of thing has happened to me from time to time over the years and I always get a smile on my face because I know God loves me and am so happy that He loves me enough to give me a little help every once in a while. Even though I am not worthy, and God owes me nothing and I owe Him everything, He still loves me enough to answer my prayers, even though sometimes I may not even be aware that I have even prayed one, to demonstrate His continued love. So, do not forget to say "thanks God" throughout the day as those unexpected gifts pop into your life.

God loves us all so much that we as humans cannot fathom the infinite reach of His goodness and love. As a spin on the Mt 16:23 verse, we as humans do not love as God does but as human beings do. Even though I try, I always find that there is some qualification or reservation to my love for God or neighbor. That is loving human style. Unconditional love is Godly love, agape love. If I could only throw the nets down and totally follow the Lord, life would be joyous and wonderful – Paradise!

The amazing revelation to come out of my prayer experience is that I knew that God knew me and loved me on a personal basis. This world has billions of people that reside on this planet. If you imagine all the people in the world standing shoulder to shoulder filling the North American Continent with me somewhere in the middle of this mass of humanity. God chose me. God knew who I was. God knew everything about me. Of the Billions of people on earth, God knows me personally and loves me so much to answer my prayers personally. The even more wonderful thing, just as Jesus knows me personally, He also knows you personally. He also loves you personally. He loves you so much that He will answer your prayers as well. He will beckon and welcome both of us individually as well as all the other billions of people on the planet are beckoned and welcomed individually to join Him in our Heavenly reward with Him eternally. It just doesn't get any better; any more amazing than that!

> *May God bless you forever, answer your prayers and fill you with His graces in accordance to His will. Amen*

## Chapter 9: God Given Gifts vs. Own Earned Wealth

I am sure you have heard or seen the monkey trap in action. This is what was used to catch monkeys in the wild successfully. What it consists of is a glass milk bottle – one with a wide enough mouth that a monkey can fit his hand through. Inside the bottle is put a nut or some sort of food that monkeys enjoy. Now the monkey comes along. At that time, the monkey has nothing, just the monkey himself. The monkey sees the food inside of the bottle and desperately wants it – not sure if the monkey just wants to have it or because it is bodily hungry. The monkey reaches inside the bottle to grab the morsel inside. Now, the monkey goes from being poor, not owning anything, to rich, owning this nice morsel of food. The monkey becomes caught when tightly gripping his treasure, can no longer fit his fist back through and out from the mouth of the milk bottle. The monkey refuses to let go of his treasure. Tug and pull, pull and tug, the monkey cannot get his fist removed from the bottle, so he can enjoy his new found wealth – the morsel.

As the monkey continues to struggle, he refuses to let the morsel go. He refuses to let go of his wealth to save himself, to get his hand back out. Therefore, the monkey's greed, to keep his treasure for himself, has now trapped him. The trappers promptly and easily walk over pick up and put the monkey into a cage, all the while the monkey continues to struggle to get his clenched fist out from the bottle and is oblivious to the fact that his now new captors have caught him and his freedom has ended. He is now an officially trapped and captive monkey specimen.

In my experience, I felt the same as the monkey with his fist stuck inside the bottle. I had so many possessions that I could not see the impending danger the weight and mass those possessions caused to impact my relationship with our Lord and my chances at Salvation. I was too busy trying to grab and hold on to all that was mine inside my bottle. I was blinded, to some extent, by the sheen of my possessions and duped into buying more to get/keep happiness rather than where I should have focused my attention – toward my Maker and Creator.

Now, I thought that I had a good relationship with Jesus. I prayed. I went to church every Sunday. I put a little something in the collection plate. Most of the time I obeyed the 10 Commandments – especially the big ones – hadn't murdered anyone; no idols of Baal in the house; no grand theft convictions. But what I did not know was that I was slowly accumulating unneeded things. Things that had "me" written all over them. Things that I "earned". Things that I bought because I felt I deserved them. Things that I bought to keep up with the times; the things that I thought would make me look good; things that at least I thought would get me noticed by the in crowd. I found that I was gravitating toward people and things while holding God at arm's length. Things, that in each one, had that component of godless mass that was accumulating and pulling me away from God.

When you look at your family's wealth that you have amassed, what do you see? How many possessions do you have? What is the gravitational pull of the worldly possessions in your life? Who owns who? Do you own your possessions or, like the monkey with a hand in the milk bottle, do your possessions own you?

I recommend that you make a list of all your possessions that you own right now. When you make this list, look at these massive amounts of possessions you own. Now, put a line through the ones you would be able to give up and live without, then, circle the ones you feel you could not live without. How many on that list would be circled? The circled items are the ones that have the most massive gravitational attraction weights. Those are the ones that tug the hardest to pull you to the other side of the room from where God lives.

Remembering back to all my family's possessions that were tossed out on and littered our lawn, our possessions on the lawn was an indictment against us that we had more stuff in our lives than we really needed or even used. The next question from the above exercise is, what are you going to do with the things that you crossed out, that you said you could live without? Would you think of possibly donating some of those to a charitable organization for someone in need to enjoy? Remember even the items that you own that you could possibly do without still have some weight attraction. The reason you keep them around is because you have some attraction to them.

There is a line in the sand with possession attraction and the Devil on one side and God and Heaven on the other. Just as one partaking in a game of tug of war, how close to that line have your possessions pulled you? How does one detach him/herself from the distractions of one's possessions, that clutters our lives, to keep well away from that line in the sand; to constantly tug oneself and pull in the direction of God's eternal graces, God's eternal reward – Salvation and Heaven? In order to joyfully and willingly be prepared to lose one's possessions if the Lord asks, one must be detached from the need to retain your worldly goods.

**Do You Possess Your Stuff Or Does Your Stuff Possess You?**

Pope Francis said the following, *"Money must serve, not rule."*[39] With this quote, substitute possessions instead of money. Possessions must serve, not rule. With all the things that you have accumulated, how much attachment do you have with those possessions? Could you bear to let a few go? How about all of them? Again, the quote from Matthew, *"Jesus said to him, 'If you wish to be perfect, go, sell what you have and give to [the] poor, and you will have treasure in heaven. Then come, follow me.' When the young man heard this statement, he went away sad, for he had many possessions."*[40] Is your treasure here with your possessions or is your treasure the Kingdom of God, Heaven?

Basically, in the case of my fire story, one might say that Jesus asked me the same question on those winter nights of prayer and prophecy prior to the fire. His question was not as drastic though as asked to the rich young man. He just asked to borrow my stuff, because I eventually, over the next several years, was able to basically get back to where I left off unfortunately. At the time I did not know I

---

[39] Pope Francis, "the Joy Of The Gospel", pg. 55
[40] Matthew 19:21-22

was ready or even consenting to lose all my possessions because the Lord did not reveal to me what the "bad thing" would be. But when the time came, my possessions did not matter. Jesus took, and I gave. So, the Jesus question to you now, if He were to exact the same request on you, what would your answer be?

The big difference between the fire and the rich young man's challenge given was, Jesus asked the young man to voluntarily dispense of his goods. I really was not given a chance to "volunteer". We have a term for that here. I was "voluntold" by the Lord.

If I was put into the young man's shoes and was told by Jesus to sell all my possessions, I would be a liar if I told you that I would have cheerfully trotted off and put up the "Yard Sale – Everything Must Go" sign in the front yard. But just the same, if the Lord were to come to me as he did and say, "I'm taking everything". I am certain now that I could answer, *"Yes Lord. Go ahead."* From my vantage point, it was much less painful to say, "ok take it" vs. "ok I will sell all my goods and give the proceeds to the poor". The Lord's foot was already well in my door at that time and the die was already cast.

How attached are you to your possessions? Enough that you would try to argue with the Lord not to take your stuff – or at least negotiate leaving a few nice ones behind? Would you answer, "Yes, per Your will Lord"? That question will have to stay a rhetorical one unless or until the Lord really puts you to a similar test. If He does, I hope He gives you the upfront grace that He gave me to answer, "Yes Lord take it all per Your will".

### How Much Is Too Much?

> *"Money has never made man happy, nor will it. There is nothing in its nature to produce happiness. The more of it one has the more one wants."*[41]

---

[41] Benjamin Franklin

Again, I recommend making an overall possessions list. When I made my list, it really opened my eyes to the excess that I and my family had amassed. As stated earlier, I initially did not think that I would be even close to my $40,000 insurance household possession limit. I did not believe I had that many possessions. My family; therefore, discovered we actually possessed a considerable amount more than our max possession limit. I had way too much stuff!

When I started to look at my list, I began to notice that I probably had not even touched 80% of my things lost in the last 5 years – maybe even longer. So that begs to ask two questions:

1. If the items are not important enough that I never use them, why were these things still in my house?

2. Why did we buy them in the first place?

How many things we buy each year that we may use one time and then park them in the garage, closet or attic? Our culture today is so impulsive that one feels he/she deserves to have that new shiny thing to make their life complete. Maybe there was a flashy ad on TV shaming you that you do not have one of these widgets so you are impelled to run out to the store just so you will not be the only person in the city without your widget.

We buy a lot of things that we absolutely do not need or at least we overbuy to have the best on the market where the average widget will do just fine. Our houses are filled to the brim with unwanted junk that seemed to be so important when purchased. We just can't let loose of them either – have to keep them and accumulate – might need that widget again someday. Some people even need to buy bigger homes to have more storage room to store their stuff.

Are you defined by your possessions? Have to have…..

- The latest super pro golf clubs

- The biggest. hottest barbecue grill (can tell I am from Texas)

- The flashiest car(s) or the most cars

- The biggest closet full of dresses and shoes – 100-year supply
- The flashiest jewelry, biggest diamond ring
- The young family with all the most up to date and most expensive stroller, car seat, baby toys…
- The biggest, fastest, most powerful computer, game system

Just look how companies such as Apple feed off this frenzy. If you do not have the latest number Apple I-Phone (5, 6, 7…) it is easy to be branded as someone that is "not normal", lives in the past with "yesterday's" cell phone – not with the in crowd. Companies like Apple and car companies are very successful with this marketing tactic. It probably would not be hard to find people that have owned every I-Phone model ever made and in the proper sequence.

When we become defined by our stuff, our stuff enslaves us – akin to the monkey's hand in the bottle. If one buys articles that serve to point the surrounding world's attention back to them, keeping them as the center of attention or at least to be noticed by the ones that are the center of attention, then those possessions do not serve to glorify God but only serves to glorify the individual. If one's happiness is defined by the quality, quantity or brand of his/her possessions, then one is never truly joyful; never satisfied; never truly free. One will always be on an eternal search mode looking for more and better stuff rather than searching for his/her salvation with his/her God, because one's stuff has become his/her god.

The sad thing is if the monkey was repatriated back into the wild, and another milk bottle placed with another treasure inside, it would draw the same monkey and the same result. We do the same thing. Continuously becoming trapped by our possessions time and time again and not able to become the person that God has created us to be.

Do you actually treat your possessions better than the people around you? *"You must remember to love people and use things, rather than to love things and use people."*[42] Do you make decisions, for instance, to play with your toys, e.g. computer equipment or watch TV instead of playing with your kids? Would you rather buy that new BMW rather than put money into your kid's college fund when your 2-year-old Dodge looks and runs just fine - all just to boast ownership in the latest luxury model with all the latest accessories and gadgets?

I am sure we all really have no idea just how many possessions we really have. That is why I recommended to make the stuff list. I was blown away by my list. Again, Cathy and I are not "high maintenance" individuals, so when I saw my list I was disappointed in myself to have so much. Again, it would be another story if I used everything on the list, but I had not touched 80% of those things in a long time. One other person may revel in their stuff list looking at their large pile of wealth accumulated as an accomplishment of some kind – I have more toys that you do mentality. The Lord does not count the number or value of your material wealth you take to your grave as a criterion to salvation. As mentioned earlier, each possession has some attachment associated to it or it would not still be in your possession – for some reason one was not able to dispense with it. The more possessions one has the bigger and stronger a magnet your possessions become to pull you closer and tighter to them, closer to that salvation line in the sand. You become a slave to your possessions. As one's stuff matters, God then fails to matter. A good rule of thumb here to abide by: it is best not to put one's self into a situation of temptation. Doing so promotes rather than prevents sin. In this case, it is best not to have excessive amounts of possessions to risk bowing to the temptation of their attractions.

An important lesson that I learned: *"The LORD gave and the LORD has taken away"*[43]. One can accumulate wealth and possessions all he/she wants. Wealth and possessions are fragile things. The Lord may just decide to pull a "Job" and take everything away. We see that happen in the news all the time – someone gets their identity stolen and the thief drains their bank account and ruins their

---

[42] Bishop Fulton J Sheen
[43] Job 1:21

credit; the stock market crashes; a fire happens, a hurricane, tornado, earthquake. *"Therefore, stay awake! For you do not know on which day your Lord will come."*[44] Or you do not know the date or time when your "fire" is coming.

Now, I would be lying to you if I were to say that our house is not filled up with possessions again. For one thing, I am writing this book on my laptop computer that I bought. So, you at least know I have one possession. But I have many more. I have gained attachment to things again. That is probably why I do not feel as close to God as I did back after the fire when I was homeless and without possessions. I look back frequently to that period of time and marvel at the joy in my life that I had when I was "poor". I truly felt the presence of the Kingdom of God on earth. I always aspire to get back to that level of Spirituality and peace.

At least I can know it is possible to be so close to God. I was there! I know what it feels like. I desperately aspire to return there. I have many fond memories and blessed lessons received of the graces that I was given during that period. This period was the best time in my life and will always be a fond memory as I grow old and gray.

I would say and hope at least that my stuff attraction level now is somewhere between pre fire and the day of the fire when I unconditionally gave up all ownership to my possessions as they were consumed. I have possessions but hopefully devote a lesser amount of attraction assigned to those things; less to pull me away from the awaiting hands of the Lord. W. C. Fields once said, *"A rich man is nothing but a poor man with money."* Poor in this case because the rich man is trapped, imprisoned by his money and possessions as he/she tries to hold tight to them to protect them from loss.

The supreme challenge issued with one's possessions is to divorce one's attraction to them. Again, possessions should serve not just to entertain and boost one's esteem and pleasure. St. Mark said in his Gospel, *"It is easier for a camel to pass through [the] eye of [a] needle*

---

[44] Matthew 24:42

*than for one who is rich to enter the kingdom of God."*[45] That detachment needed for a rich person to divorce himself from allegiance to his possessions is the toughest challenge there is. To have possessions and not be drawn to them; to pay no allegiance to your worldly goods; to possess a habitual and unconditionally generous heart, can only be done with the radical grace of God, and the courage and willingness to ask for and cooperate with it. To be able and willing to share and give it all up and to follow Jesus will be the rhetorical question that we all must be able to answer in God's favor.

If there is one thing that one gleans from this story is this: Your job on this earth is not to accumulate the most and best possessions one can by the end of your life. Your challenge is to get to Heaven. God does not take a possession inventory when you stand in front of Him at the Pearly Gates. One does not get extra credit points for having the best and greatest things. God wants a pure heart. A heart without attractions and allegiances to other gods, for instance, a big bank account, a fancy new car or a big and lavish house. Jesus wants you. He wants your loving heart to be entwined with His. If one only takes this advice to heart, my book will have accomplished what it was intended to do.

> *Lord give me a clean heart. A heart free from the worldly distractions of wealth and materialism. May You be my all, my everything. May You and You alone be my God, my Savior, my King and my way of life, leading me to my just rewards in Heaven with You for ever and ever. Amen.*

---

[45] Mark 10:25

## Chapter 10: We Take A Lot Of Things For Granted

One of the eye opening occurrences encountered those first days after the fire was, how many things, each that played some part of my everyday life, were then missing? Consumed by the fire. I did not realize that I was even missing them, until the time of the day arrived that I normally used them. They were gone, no longer available to me. A good example was that first morning after I woke up from my brief rest after the fire. My first thought was, "I would like to brush my teeth." I quickly realized that I no longer had a tooth brush or even tooth paste to be able to accomplish that task. This started a string of humbling realizations of all these little things that I depended on to get through my daily routine, that were now gone. I never thought of these items as being important, but instantly realized how important a role each played, in their little way, to assist my walk of life through my day. When missing, there was a little pot hole in my day that I had to negotiate around. The day's routine was crimped and interrupted as I now had to take my day off from "automatic pilot" to work around these new holes in my routine.

Here is another task. Starting in the morning when you wake up, make a list of all the things that you use and come into contact with during the day. From the alarm clock that you turn off to your morning newspaper. List your shower and hygiene products used. List your toothbrush, toothpaste, socks, clothing, shoes you wear etc. Continue on through the day. How many things do you use that are so automatic in nature, in your day, that you unthinkingly and unconsciously breeze through the day, not even acknowledging their use or existence? Now, how would your day go if some of these "routine" items were removed?

Even after making a list, it may be difficult to really appreciate these items until one or more are actually missing from your day. As stated above, that is what happened to my family during our fire experience. When one is truly poor as my family was that morning of the fire, these normal conveniences and day to day necessities to our normal lives, were now missing and, for the first time, were sorely missed. Their new found importance gave them a much higher priority and value as they were no longer in my life and available for use or consumption.

For instance, I do not ever remember being without a pair of shoes to wear. I always had multiple changes of clothes. I have never had to beg for a place to house my family. After contemplating our poorness that morning, I realized how much I took these normal routine staples for granted. I never looked at them before as items that I should be grateful for because they were automatic. They were always there.

Starting the morning of the fire, and as the waves of people rushed to us donating these simple necessities, I gained an all new appreciation for these simple day to day items. They no longer were something automatic because for the first time, they were missing. I could not go to the drawer and pull out a pair of socks. Not only did I not have any socks to my name, I did not have a drawer either. In those first several days, we had to rely on the generosity of our fellow brothers and sisters to provide each and every standard living component – clothes, food, a place to cook food, things to eat on and with, a phone, a roof over our heads, a place to sleep and take a shower etc.

Before the fire, I do not remember ever thanking the Lord for all these minor necessities I encountered daily. I never thanked the Lord for my tooth brush, for instance. I never thanked the Lord for a bed to sleep on. I never assigned values to these items before in life because they were always there for the using and not even a thought that they would not be there every time I needed them. Just think how much we should be thankful for. Thankful for the things we really lack gratitude to our Lord for because they have become automatic in our daily routine. It caught me by surprise how grateful my family and I really were to the people that donated these everyday items the days after the fire. Those items, once taken for granted, seemed to have taken an all new and high value now that they were gone.

One thing I would suggest is, volunteer and serve at a homeless area or shelter. I am not suggesting to go with the mindset to be thankful for what you have vs. the meager possessions these homeless people have. The objective here is not to celebrates one's fortunes. What one can see, by watching homeless people rifle through donated items brought, is the intense and pure joy they get when finding that pair of socks or a belt. I remember the first time I saw the reaction of an individual's joy when picking up a pair of socks I had donated. I was really taken back at the level of excitement shown by the person for an item that I definitely took for granted. Something I saw as of low value because, at that time, I had a plethora of pairs of socks in my drawers. Everyone has plenty of socks, right? Not a homeless person though. If one wants to really see people that do not take these little things for granted, these are the people. When one has nothing, even what we envision as a routine, normal and every day item, to them is viewed with a high sense of value. There is excitement and genuine gratitude when a homeless person receives such a gift. This is how grateful we all need to be; to celebrate every gift from God, the great and the small.

In another thought, what about the people in your life that you come into contact with each day? How grateful are you for all the people you have in your life? How grateful are you for your family? I know after I experienced a real situation where I stood a good chance to lose them, I gained an all new love and value for my family members. I am hoping all have a fond and genuine love and give thanks each day for one's family. What about your boss? How about that person at work that drives you crazy? How about all the people that you walk past and bump into each day? Each one of these people somehow and in some way, touches your life. Each person you come into contact in some way, see walking down the sidewalk, or when driving by, makes your life better and more complete – even people that you may not get along with. One probably does not think to thank God for all these ancillary people that touch your life's periphery.

For instance, there is an elderly gentleman that every morning walks the street in front of our church picking up trash. Every morning when I drive by him, he gives me a big smile and a wave. He does the same for every car that passes. That gesture brightens my whole day. I am greatly thankful for this man in my life.

Now, what about the poor people in your city? What about the homeless people in your area? What about the immigrants that are pouring across our borders? What about the Down Syndrome young man in your neighborhood? How thankful are we about and for them? Do we instead wish they would just go away or disappear because they make us feel uncomfortable? This is where our true charity and love needs to grow and envelop our poor and disadvantaged, to embrace them as true sons and daughters of God as we all are. We are mandated by Jesus to love our neighbors. The first part of loving your neighbors is to be thankful for them.

I feel that there is a connection between the attachments of our goods with how much we take things for granted. If we are thankful for each and every item that we own – give it to God, realize all came from God – we would not, have attachments to our possessions. The more items we take for granted, the more these items enslave us. If we take for granted that we will always have clothes is one level. If we take for granted that we have and deserve really nice clothes, then our level of attachment grows exponentially.

When one hears a commercial that states that "you deserve" this product, basically the message is telling you that this item is so normal in the scheme of things that you should take it for granted that you should have this item. Just look at what we now consider as normal living possessions we now have and take for granted vs. 10 or 20 or 30 years ago. Our things we take for granted continue to complicate our lives and enslave us.

I remember 50 years ago, it was a luxury to have first a black and white TV, then a color TV. Now it would be strange to see a home without a color TV in every room, with cable. Not only do we have a home computer, everyone in the family now has at least one computer device. Let's not even talk about cell phones.

We need to view our possessions with gratitude. Gratitude first, that the Lord put in place the individuals that were smart and talented enough to invent those things, but also be grateful to God for the gifts He has put into our lives. As stated in the prior chapter, we need to question and challenge our purchases to minimize the number of things that detract from our worship of God. We need to be good stewards of our wealth and allocate our funds to serve God and not us. We need to be thankful to God for everything we have and own because it all came from Him. We deserve nothing, but God in His infinite love for us gives us all we have. So, when you see a commercial that implores you to buy some widget because you "deserve it", just remember, you don't. Evaluate how you will serve God by making such a purchase. Those things that a company says you "deserve" are probably ones that go into the closet after a couple of uses, or of all the advertised gadgets that the car had, you never use them and could have purchased a less expensive car with fewer gadgets (or not buy the car in the first place because your current one is just fine).

Do you own your possessions or do your possessions own you? Who does your possessions serve – you or God?

> *May you always thank God for each and every possession that you have from the greatest to the least. May you be able to unconditionally part with and share your possessions and wealth with those in need, showing your possessions have no hold over you. May your possessions help you glorify our Lord and Savior and bring you closer to your entry into God's Kingdom in Heaven. Amen.*

## Chapter 11: The Essence Of True Peace

How can one be silent when one finds the Lord's peace? St. Therese of Lisieux once said, *"Let us go forward in peace, our eyes upon heaven, the only one goal of our labors."* But truly, if one finds the source of blissful peace from the Lord, why would one not burst to tell everyone. Well, let me try, because it isn't easy. Again, these human and English words cause problems because there are not enough or glorious enough words to really do the topic justice.

As mentioned during my discussion about my conversations with God, both in my pre fire and at the fire scene itself, one gift that I was consistently given at each occasion was a deep cleansing feeling of the Lord's peace. This was the main validation that these individual events were real and were Heaven sent.

The feeling of peace received was comparable to no other feeling of comfort or joy received from doing earthly things. It felt as if the room was filled with peace. I do not know if any of you have ever experienced stepping into a soundproof room before. When one steps from the loud and bustling outside and then into that sound proof room, one gets a strange feeling or sensation as your new environment includes almost zero sound. The only sound in the room is of you moving and breathing. It is as if the entire world other than you has been evacuated from this new world you stand in.

The sensation of peace that I received was somewhat similar in comparison. It was as if all distraction was removed to distract peace. The room was quiet and peaceful because all kids and Cathy were upstairs sleeping, but when the feeling of cleansing peace came rolling in, it took that peace in the room to a whole another level. All that was left in my being, after my prayer sessions with God ended, was His total peace.

When the feeling of peace came, it felt like all my cares and worries melted away and were gone. This was truly amazing since the message the Lord had given me involved that something disastrous was about to happen to my family. At all times through this message, I was calm and knew the Lord was with me so there was nothing I should fear (e.g. 23rd Psalm). I felt the Lord's peace during the messages, but when the message was over – Wow! The peace just seemed to roll in. The feeling I had was similar to that of being rolled out by a rolling pin as it wrung out all my cares and worries, especially any left over from the Lord's message. It was all gone.

This level of peace really prepared me for the eventual day of the fire. It almost seemed natural that day when I equated tragedy with peace and that all was right by God, just part of His plan. I also had a strong feeling that the Lord would repay my troubles far more than what troubles we were about to experience. After the prayer preparation sessions ended, I was well prepared to do God's will whatever it was that He had planned for me and family.

The day of the fire, the feeling of peace was again cleansing, just as during the preparation sessions. As mentioned in the fire story, I could feel the weight of my possessions and their attachments oozing out from my body. Again, similar to the rolling pin analogy, I could feel the weight of my possessions being rolled out and out from my body. I felt lighter. I felt as if I could almost float. I had joy at losing my possessions.

I am sure that my neighbors and the firemen there thought I was loony. They all expected to see a tearful bucket of mush when they came to console me. I must say I was tearful, but tears of joy. Once I figured out that the fire was the bad thing God predicted to happen, a level of peace, that intuitively I should not have had, enveloped me. It was still hard standing and watching my home burn because that is where we lived and loved. That is where we broke bread and prayed. There would be no more good memories made in that house.

A third level or time of peace received was watching God's plan unfold. Once the Lord clued me in to what was happening as the area's new philanthropists began their acts of charity and mercy towards us, all I did then was sit back and watch the play unfold in front of me. I had first, the peace of mind that we would be ok. We would be well taken care of. All I had to do was be God's conduit for all these great people to let their pent up mercy explode. I was allowed to see Jesus every day, multiple times, as people came to give assistance. I really did see Jesus in their eyes because their eyes were so radiant when their charity was being shed.

I must add that doing God's work and will, in itself, is a very peaceful thing. It gave me a wonderful feeling of peace just to be able to give the show to God and not worry what part I had to play, or worry that I would mess up or poison God's plan. God took all that away from me and all I did was watch, smile and bask in the Lord's love and peace.

One of the most peaceful and joyful of these visits came from one of my CRHP brothers that was a part of my first presentation team. He had lost his job the year before and when Christmas came around, they did not have money to buy their four kids presents. So, our CRHP brothers got together and put together some toys and books for the kids. Among those were toys and board games that my family donated to the cause. I purchased a Santa suit (which was one of the casualties of the fire). After pulling together presents for the family, several of us from the CRHP team went to deliver the presents with me dressed as Santa. The look on those kids' faces and the gratitude on mom and dad's face was incredible.

Well, come fire time, who should show up but the same guy returning the toys and board games to my kids since they no longer had any toys left. There was some hugging and tears of gratitude on both sides. My friend, having a chance to return the favor from the Christmas before, and me in total gratitude now that the shoe was on the other foot. I am not sure who coined the phrase that to know someone you have to walk in the other's shoes first. Well, here were two fellows that had now walked in each other's shoes – both on the needy and on the charitable sides. That was a special day.

One major lesson learned over the course of the fire episode was, peace is not earned. One cannot buy peace. One cannot put together a plan of action to end up with peace. Peace just happens. It is given – a gift from God and not earned. It happens with total agape love. It happens by totally giving yourself, your total being, to God – "Do with me what you need. I am yours." Those are 9 of the toughest words to get out of one's mouth in prayer. One steps into the vast unknown by uttering those 9 words. He may just take everything from you. He may call you to go or do something that totally scares you to your core. But if you submit to your loving Creator and God, the rewards are life changing, unimaginably magnificent. The Lord will answer your prayers in a way that cannot be comprehended.

A quote from Mother Teresa used earlier in the book summarizes the feelings when stepping out with the Lord. *"I know God won't give me anything I can't handle. I just wish he didn't trust me so much."* I felt the same way through this fire process. One thing I have learned is to be prepared what you ask God for. You might just have your prayer answered in the most radical way. Radical ways are most scary, but they also come with huge rewards.

In Franklin D Roosevelt's first inaugural speech, he uttered the now immortal words: *"The only thing to fear is fear itself."* FDR's quote is backed up by the following quotes:

- St. Pope John Paul II: *"And usually it is then that fears and doubts come to disturb us and make it more difficult to decide. It is then that we need to hear the Lord's Assurance: 'I am with you'"*

- Pope Benedict XVI: *"Do not be afraid of Christ! He takes nothing away and he gives you everything. When we give ourselves to him, we receive a hundredfold in return."*

- Psalm 27:1: *"The Lord is my light and my salvation; whom should I fear? The Lord is my life's refuge; of whom should I be afraid?"*

- Psalm 46:11: *"Be still and know that I am God"*

If the Lord is with us, what can go wrong? Who can be against us? Peace starts with shedding one's shackles that are holding him/her back from attaining God's will for us. Again, to throw down your nets and follow Christ. In a sermon of Pope Francis' during his 2015 trip to South America, he challenged us to bring out our absolute best to the world for Jesus.

If we aspire to look to find peace we are complicating the formula too much and will fall short. Peace does not happen by somehow executing a plan to bring external things in our life and in the world into equilibrium, harmony. Peace comes from within. Peace comes from reconciling one's self to the will of God. The key is, always aspire to work to love and serve God in everything we do. To give God our best. To do the simple things with love. Here is Mother Teresa's list for the road to peace – The Simple Path:

*"<u>The Simple Path</u>*
*Silence is Prayer*
*Prayer is Faith*
*Faith is Love*
*Love is Service*
*The Fruit of Service is Peace"*

*I pray that you always find your peace by saying "Yes" to Jesus whenever He asks to use you as His instrument of Salvation. Amen*

## Chapter 12: Paid Back In Full

> *"Jesus said, 'Amen, I say to you, there is no one who has given up house or brothers or sisters or mother or father or children or lands for my sake and for the sake of the gospel who will not receive a hundred times more now in this present age: houses and brothers and sisters and mothers and children and lands, with persecutions, and eternal life in the age to come.'"*[46]

You know, it is hard to keep up with an infinite being. Here I already owe God my entire life and I am trying to repay Him for all that I have that He has given me. All these years heading up to the fire, I tried to do my best to give of my time, talent and treasure whenever He called me to do so. Then Jesus goes and gives me another infinite dose of gifts that I can never hope to repay Him for. How wonderful is our God?!

I remember a conversation I had with my Grandfather Spindler when I was young. Every time we would visit and stay over at their house, my grandfather, at one or more times throughout the visit, volunteered in some capacity, helping out at church. One day, I asked him why he did so much for the Church. He answered me, *"John, I am not a wealthy man. I could never afford to contribute enough money to repay God's kindness, so that is why I volunteer my time to help give back to God for all his kindness and love He has given to us."* You know, however hard he worked, he never was able to pay back what he owed. To his credit, my sainted 97-year-old grandfather died trying though.

As my grandfather lived his life, it is not important how close one gets to being even with God, because you will never ever get close. What is important is that one consistently puts one's Faith in action when approached by God to do His will. As Jesus said, *"Not everyone*

---

[46] Mark 10:29-30

who says to me, 'Lord, Lord,' will enter the kingdom of heaven,- but only the one who does the will of my Father in heaven."[47] As stated by the epistle of James, *"Faith of itself, if it does not have works, is dead."*[48] What is important is to demonstrate your love and Faith in Jesus by hearing His Words and saying "Yes" to His calls for action; to participate in your and the world's plan for salvation that God has for us.

Another trap is to say to yourself, "The Lord's gifts are so infinite in magnitude, I will never get close to repaying Him, so why bother?" Again, God is beckoning each one of us to participate in a relationship with Him. To be in a relationship with Jesus, we need to be involved in our own Salvation. We need to say "Yes" to God when called. If we fail to use the opportunities that God puts before us every day to participate in our Salvation, then He will indeed spit out those lukewarm "good Christians" (see Revelations 3:15-16). He will say, *"I never knew you. Depart from me, you evildoers."*[49] There is one reason why a person would consistently consent to refuse to cooperate with calls given to do God's will, regardless what one says about his/her affiliation with God – and that reason is: the person really does not possess a deep love for God.

As one becomes aware and acts on callings from God, this brings that person closer to the glory and goodness of the Lord. It also brings the individual to be the best that God has created the person to be. The number of works performed is not something to track or gauge. God's works completed serve as a personal growth path, a journey, to attain Spiritual greatness under the eyes of our Lord. The question of importance is, when the Lord calls and asks you to participate in his will, what and how do you answer that calling? Do you ignore the call and maybe it will go away? Do you flat out tell the Lord, "No"? Do you come up with excuses to try to justify opting out of a calling?

We all at times give all three of those types of answers to God's callings, unfortunately. It is embarrassing, looking back on some

---

[47] Matthew 7:21
[48] James 2:17
[49] Matthew 7:23

occasions where my Lord and Savior, that has given me everything including my life and existence here on earth, has asked me to do something for Him and I unceremoniously and flat out turned Him down. How could I do such a thing to my Creator who has been so generous and loving to me? I am sorry to say that I have turned my Lord and Savior down on many occasions.

We humans are so fortunate to have a loving and eternally compassionate God who continues to lavish us with His calls to do His will and allow us to grow in Him toward our Salvation. We owe Him an infinite debt that we would never be capable to pay back. We; therefore, owe it to our Lord to listen and heed His calls whenever and wherever we hear and recognize them; to not only say "Yes" but to say "Yes" unconditionally and with joy. One must resemble those people that came to our aid with glowing eyes that were so excited to be able to help their neighbor in need.

It is not that God needs our services to help save the world. He could do that with a bat of His eye. In conjunction with and even despite our free will, God has established His plan for our and the world's Salvation to include the participation of us humans. Therefore, it is up to us to cooperate with God's will and callings to participate in the world's salvation as well as our own.

The Chomistek house fire was an example of a multiple calling opportunity situation. First the Chomisteks were asked and said "Yes, let it be done according to His word." Do to our "Yes", God sent invitations out to the people living in the Castleton and Lawrence township area to participate in His will to provide charity to a neighbor in need. Now some of the people, I do not know how many, said "No" or "let someone else help them out", or "No, I do not know them". But hundreds of people said, "Yes, I will do your will and help the Chomistek family in any way I can." Now, in light of the Good Samaritan Parable, Jesus then asks, *"Which of these in your opinion was neighbor to the Chomisteks?"*[50] Which of these people then

---

[50] Luke 10:36

worked, in conjunction with their calling by God, to participate in their and the world's salvation?

The fire situation is one example of single and multiple calling opportunities that are given every day to each one of us. It is up to us to first, recognize the opportunity that God is calling us for, secondly, to say "Yes", lastly, the action is performed, as required, to complete the "Yes". Your "Yes" is so important in God's plan, even though it may look tiny in your eyes, because your "Yes" may be the first calling in a series of events such as our fire event. If I refused God's will and the fire somehow failed to materialize because of my refusal, God would not have been able to send out the other invitations to the people around us to get involved with the prayer that was our fire ministry. Your "Yes" to Jesus could start a major reaction of "Yes's" that could end up energizing the country, or even the world.

In order for us to continue to search out Jesus to work toward our Salvation, we need to continue to search out for His callings and continue to answer "Yes" vs. some sort of excuse to decline. A person who only resorts to helping friends and helping only when convenient to do so would fall into the lukewarm category. I tell you what, I never want to go before the Lord and have Him spit me out!

There are two responsibilities involved in your "Yes" to God. The first is to say, "Yes". The second responsibility is to perform the action with joy and gladness. As in the Parable of the two sons (found in Matthew 21:28-32), even though one brother initially says "No", or grumbles but then does the will of the Father, the Father's will does get done. On the other hand, if one does the work with joy and gladness, the value of that work and the person's reward will be greater toward one's salvation. With each completed "Yes", one grows their Christian character to a higher level of virtue. We may not always achieve the total enveloping level of joy and peace every time we go about doing God's bidding, but we will always attain a noticeable level of God's joy and peace, as the reward, when completing each one of the Lord's given tasks.

So, in summary, in order to keep on one's path, trending toward our and the world's salvation, we need to continue to be vigilant, to heed and answer "Yes" to the Lord's biddings. One never has enough goodness in one's bank to ever justify passing on any opportunity God presents to us to do His will. There is also a high responsibility to say "Yes" to God because the salvation of many other brothers and sisters in Christ may also be in your hands. By saying "No" to Christ, you may be negating the causal opportunities, invitations God had planned to give to many others, robbing them of salvific graces those others could have merited.

When the Lord energized our communities surrounding my family after the fire, He heaped another infinite dose of His gifts on my family and me. Likewise, God also heaped an infinite dose of grace to all those that came to our aid as well. As Psalm 116:12 states, *"How can I repay the LORD for all the great good done for me?"* Again, even though I have no means in my human limitations to ever come close to repaying Jesus, just for the gifts given during the fire experience alone, the best I can do is, learn to love Jesus even better and more completely than before; by heeding and answering every possible call He gives to me. I need to grow more fervent with my prayer life to build a closer relationship with Jesus and the Holy Spirit, to first, be able to hear and recognize His calls, then pray for the Faith and courage to step out and say, "Yes, I will do whatever you ask of me." If I do not, I may never hear those cherished words from Jesus upon our meeting at the Pearly Gates of Heaven, *"Well done, my good and faithful servant....Come, share your master's joy."*[51]

> *I pray that you recognize God's voice when you see a person in need; to see Jesus in that person; to act with mercy and kindness; to share God's gifts that were given to you with your fellow brother in Christ in need. I pray that you find the Lord's peace and joy in everything you do. Amen*

---

[51] Matthew 25:21

## Chapter 13: Doing God's Will Breeds Disciples

When looking back on what transpired that first week after the fire, one question that jumped out was the following, "Who was being a disciple of Christ and who was the recipient of discipleship? I saw discipleship play out as a two-way street. During an encounter when a person would visit to deliver their charitable contribution to us, the discipleship meter seemed to be a swinging pivot. First, the discipleship meter pointed to them and then back to me then back again. From my experience, during those hours and days of the fire story, discipleship really bread and fed on the discipleship being shared during the encounter. The more I just let the Lord's business be done, the more of His discipleship developed in both the people I came into contact with as well as within myself. As the discipleship bounced between the two of us, I could feel God's presence within that discipleship encounter grow and grow to a feverish level. By the time the person left, I could tell that the person was filled with joy and God's fervor. I was bubbling in the Lord as well.

What does it mean to be a true disciple of Jesus? What does it mean to truly live out one's Faith – Faith in action? Jesus mentions numerous times throughout the Bible reminding and giving us examples through His parables how we are to live and share our Faith in God; to spread Jesus' love and Church to the world; to be His disciples. The Good Samaritan Parable[52] provides a prime look at both what Jesus is expecting a disciple to look and act like, as well as the opposite, the example of one behaving in opposition to Jesus' rule. How a discipleship act plays out causes God's Word to either spread out to the world or can actually cause it to shrink and hide depending on whether the act becomes a positive or negative display of discipleship.

In this story the Samaritan steps out of his cultural set of rules, out of compassion, to assist a Jew who was lying beaten upon the side of the road. The Samaritan risked condemnation by both his people as well as the Jews in order to minister to the needs of this injured person. He showed true discipleship by risking everything to do God's will.

---

[52] Luke 10:29-37

The fruits of his discipleship would be magnified as his compassion and charity was witnessed and experienced by both the man in need as well as the innkeeper who the Samaritan pressed into service to take care of the injured man. Both now would have been deeply impressed and affected by the example (seed planted) of the compassion and charity demonstrated by the Samaritan. This display of compassion would encourage the Samaritan's brave model of discipleship to be copied and carried outward with them to share that charity experienced to others the two met. This showing of discipleship and mercy thus brings all three, the Samaritan, the beaten person and inn keeper, to a fuller closeness to God and their salvation due to the actions of one person – The Samaritan. Discipleship breeds more discipleship.

Now on the other hand, two prominent Jews walked right past the injured man because they were afraid and/or unwilling to risk touching a bleeding, injured person thus be singled out per the Jewish law as "being unclean". They failed to comply with God's calling for mercy at the expense of compliance to a manmade law. Their example given to all who may have witnessed this undertaking, especially the beaten man, was, "the law trumps God". If not for the charitable actions by the Samaritan, their bad example would have had a negative effect on the faith journeys of all that were involved; the opposite direction needed to seek God and His Salvation.

The main task for a disciple of Jesus is to have the fortitude to step out to spread Jesus' love to one's neighbors; to heed Jesus' calling no matter the perceived cost. As the Samaritan did, a disciple of Jesus is not afraid to step out and use his/her talents, chancing losing everything to gain everything by following Jesus and heeding His calls to do His will. In this case, the Samaritan spread the Word of God by his charitable actions.

The people that physically came out to visit and comfort my family after the fire had to put their Faith and egos on the line. There was no assurance of what type of reception they would get from me as far as my accepting or embracing their act of mercy shared. They had to step out into the unknown and take that first step to be a disciple for Christ;

to be willing to step into a personal encounter with another human being; to put one's Faith on the line and personally encounter another person, perceived in need, to share their compassion and charity. These people took the gifts that God had given them and by giving them away and sharing their discipleship; they parlayed those gifts into much more – a community full of compassion and charity – of discipleship. They returned home that day with considerably more "Jesus" in their hearts and lives than they had when starting the day. They were paid 100 fold for their discipleship and charity given.

In order to meet the discipleship challenge, one must be willing and able to share your gifts and talents; to share and present Jesus to the world. It is an interesting play on words, maybe a coincidence, that the word "Talents" used in the Parable of Talents[53] can be viewed both in its money/treasure aspect – the Roman currency – as well as talents of one's personal abilities. Both are given by God for us to glorify Him with.

God has given everyone, especially my readers of this book, many talents. Personal talents are also wealth, one can argue. Talents are actionable wealth that allows each of us individually and as groups to influence the world positively or negatively as our talents are either used or not used properly. God gave us natural born talents that we grew up with. He also continues to lavish additional gifts of talents on us as we go through life. These talents are given to supplement the gifts we already have to allow us to manage what God has in mind for us, our special tasks given us to do our part to fulfill His master plan for the world. An example of a gift of talents received might be the ability to withstand the supreme challenge of losing all one's possessions in a house fire and to use that loss to evangelize and empower a community.

As Jesus said in the Book of Luke, *"Much will be required of the person entrusted with much, and still more will be demanded of the person entrusted with more."*[54] God has entrusted so many blessings and talents on us all that we are not capable to comprehend and

---

[53] Matthew 25:14-30
[54] Luke 12:48

recognize them all. God gives us marching orders to be disciples of His and share that wealth of talents with our neighbors in Christ. When we come up against a calling, a challenge given by God to do a work that seems way out of one's capability to perform, I am betting that you have some hidden talents given by God that if cultivated, tried and used, one can do what now seems impossible. In the last century, we have seen some pretty amazing feats accomplished through and by very ordinary people that had no history or pre-qualifications that would make them viable candidates to accomplish the lofty goals they were actually able to achieve. Just look at examples such as St. Pope John Paul II's role in the fall of communism in Russia. He did what all the ICBM nuclear missiles in the US aimed at Russia could not. Look at Mother Teresa and her work in India and around the world to care for the hopeless. Look at Mother Angelica who created a global Catholic radio and television network (EWTN) with no electronic or broadcasting industry aptitude or experience to start out with. God calls and God equips.

Another question that can be asked is, "Do you see the talents, that you at least recognize and are aware that you have, as have been given to you by God, or do you see them as something that you have earned or cultivated on your own?" If talents are not seen as blessings coming from God, one first sells him/herself short of what one is capable to undertake, but one also lacks the compassion and humility to be a disciple, to enter into and say "Yes" to perform God's will and callings.

Odds are very high that each one of us falls heavily into the *"entrusted with much"* category and again pretty high odds that we are in the even higher *"entrusted with more"* one. To meet the expectation of our Maker, one must first realize that all talents we have are gifted by God, then be thankful and realize that you have all the talents given to you necessary for doing God's bidding and will. After realizing all talents do come from God, one must feel empowered and obligated to share and use those talents to glorify God – do His will – to be His disciple; to drop the nets and follow. That is what a disciple is and does. There should be no reason to turn down a calling from God. You can do it!

**Cannot Stop Being A Disciple**

So, after the fire business subsided, there was a natural tendency to let my discipleship guard down. A justifiable reaction here could have been for family and me to assume that, "The fire was the thing that we were put on this earth to do or endure to win our Salvation; therefore, we fulfilled all what God had asked us do and were officially 'saved'." I must admit, that it took me a while to realize, but God was not through with us yet. He was just getting started. Maybe that is why He sent the wrong way semi-truck my way several months later.

It really took me about 10 years to again feel comfortable enough to reinvestigate discipleship to be able to get up the courage to listen for and be able to ask the Lord for additional ways to fulfill His bidding. Prior to that, and still to this day, I still cringe a bit when I contemplate what God is asking me to do. I guess I have had firsthand experiences to know that I need to be prepared for anything from the whisper of the gentle breeze to the earthquake when God calls. God may call me to something radical, way out of my box of comfort. He may just call me to give someone a smile and a hand shake.

The first real call that I responded to was about the year 2005. I have always had a love for the Priesthood and in some respects, was disappointed that God had not called me there. I am ecstatic with my married life Vocation, but from time to time I still have a passing thought, if the cards fell a little differently, I might be saying Masses rather than designing boxes and bottles.

As mentioned earlier, after the fire, my family moved to Plano, TX in 1998. In 2001 the initial parish in Plano we had joined, St. Elizabeth Seton, became a huge mega parish which was split up into two parishes (old and new) to ease the overcrowding at St. E's facilities and Masses – especially during Christmas and Easter. On those Holy Days, St. Elizabeth would have so many people attend the Christmas and Easter Masses, that there were often satellite rooms in the education building set up to handle the many overflow crowd where parishioners there had to watch the Mass on TV. The Priests, Deacons or Extraordinary Ministers of the Eucharist would then make the rounds with Holy Communion to each classroom after finishing with the parishioners that were lucky enough to find a seat or standing room in the church proper.

Our family joined the new parish, Our Lady of Angels (OLA). We were one of the founding members for the new parish. I was involved at the new parish as an Extraordinary Eucharistic Minister but that was really the extent of my involvement at the time. Around the year 2005, I began to feel a calling to do something to promote the Priesthood at the parish. I checked the ministry list at OLA and found there was no listing for a Vocations Awareness ministry. As the parish was still new, the parish was still early in its process to develop, set up and establish the various ministries normally found at a fully established parish. God began to tug at my mind. I was sure that I was not the ministry leadership type. I prayed and listened. God tugged. God was imploring me to jump back into discipleship mode to fulfill something that He was calling me all these years to do for Him.

Finally, I got the courage to approach Monsignor Bell, our pastor, to inquire about starting a Vocations Awareness ministry at the parish. I guess this time; I was the one that played the part of the lady asking who she should write the check to. Without batting an eye, Msgr. Bell agreed and instantly I was an OLA ministry head. I was now a "fisher of men"[55]. This time the Lord did not require any radical loss of physical things, he was looking for a radical change to my Faith and discipleship. He wanted me to be a Vocations seed planter.

My first challenge was to figure out what a Vocations Awareness Ministry is and does. I interviewed several Vocations Awareness directors at other parishes in the area and found one program in common at most of the parishes visited, which was a weekly family prayer for Vocations program run at Sunday Masses. Parishioner volunteers were secured for each Sunday Mass to come up in front of

---

[55] Mark 1:17

church at the end of Mass to accept the commission to pray as a family for Vocations over that next week. Family Prayers for Vocations was a powerful tool to put into place.

At the time the OLA Vocation Awareness Ministry was to begin the promotion of Religious Vocations, promoting Vocations was not the most popular of topics. The year of 2005 was right at the height of the priest pedophile scandal. I was about to ask families to pray for their sons and daughters to enter into a Vocation to the Priesthood and Consecrated Religious life when Religious Vocations were not on parents' top list of possible Vocation choices they would encourage for their children to pursue. Not only that, the Priesthood actually made many parent's list of those Vocations they did not want their children to pursue. Even though, I felt the Lord calling me to establish the program.

So, I started the OLA Family Prayer for Vocation program. The program was designed to run during the school year then took breaks during Advent and Lenten seasons. The Prayers for Vocation program cemented my mission, asking families to pray together as a family unit for at least one week for Vocations and also for our Priests and Religious.

As it turned out, through a seed planted by this program, I discovered a second parallel calling that seemed to "accidentally" appear. Not only could this program promote prayer for Vocations, it could also promote prayer in general with and within the family unit. What I did not fathom was, through this calling to establish a Vocations Awareness Ministry, the Lord was again adding a new calling for me – to be an active disciple to the parish.

Through the Vocations Awareness Ministry, I was planting seeds to entice others to take on discipleship roles by encouraging parents to promote and lead prayers in their homes as a family unit. I did not want to think of myself as a disciple because, as I thought, discipleship is what the Priests and Nuns do. Regardless how I felt and what I thought I was doing, I had again become a disciple for the Lord.

# I Have Come To Set The Earth On Fire

God continued to work in me to plant more seeds through this ministry to promote other things to build His Kingdom here at Our Lady of Angels. A second prayer program that was started through the Vocations Awareness Ministry was the daily Mass Rosary devotion. Other more established parishes had a before or after daily Mass Rosary devotion. Our young parish did not have such a program yet. Since the Family Prayer for Vocations program took a "vacation" during Lent, I looked for ways to carry on prayer for Vocations during the Lenten season. So, a Lenten Rosary for Vocations was started after the Saturday morning Mass each week during Lent.

I remember the first Saturday's Rosary. There was only four people present that Saturday in the temporary chapel OLA had. I could really feel the Spiritual energy though in that small chapel room as we said our first Rosary together as a parish function. I played a Rosary CD that my mom sent me recorded by the Bishop of the Saginaw, Michigan Diocese, Bishop Robert Carlson, which was recorded with his diocesan seminarians. It had a Vocations tone and at the start of each decade, the Bishop would provide a short talk relating the decade's mystery to a Vocational calling experience. I am not sure if the Spiritual energy in the room was the cause, but on the wall, was mounted a wood holder that held a small glass bowl with Holy Water. As we were in one of the latter mysteries of that Rosary, all of a sudden, we heard a loud snapping noise. Looking toward the Holy Water bowl on the wall, where the noise had originated, the glass bowl it held split in two pieces. That's the power of the Spirit!

The Lenten Rosary for Vocations went on for two years. The program planted another seed. OLA parishioners wanted the opportunity to say the Rosary year round. I next received a request from the OLA's Knights of Columbus Grand Knight to initiate a monthly Rosary program. So, the Lenten Rosary program was expanded to every first Saturday of every month. At this date (2015), the Rosary program seed planted has now germinated and was expanded by other parishioner disciples taking the charge. Now a Rosary is said six days a week prior to every weekday and Saturday morning Mass. In addition, another Rosary is said after the 9:00am

Mass on Sundays as well. Still another family started an annual event where a Rosary is said in multiple languages to celebrate the universality of the Catholic Faith and the ethnic diversity of our parish. Discipleship again breeds more discipleship.

The Rosary program is another good example of seeds planted by way of Christ and the Holy Spirit through its humble beginning as a Vocations Awareness program. The first seed was the birth of a Vocations Awareness Ministry. Second, the initiation of the Family Prayer for Vocations program that promoted both prayer for Vocations and established a promotion of prayer as a family unit at parishioner homes. The next seed saw the establishment of Our Lady's Rosary first, during Lent, then expanding as more disciples got involved to establish a program where at least one Rosary is now said 365 days a year at OLA. I am glad to say that the parish produced its first Seminarian this year. The Seminarian came from one of the first families that volunteered for the Family Prayer for Vocations program back in 2006.

Since Pope Francis has been our Pontiff, he has pushed the Intentional Discipleship initiative started by St. Pope John Paul II and his predecessor Pope Paul VI. He is bringing to light that the mission of the Church is Missionary Discipleship. The challenge now to the Church as well as to me is, how can we become better, more complete, and more radical intentional disciples for Christ?

The first thing that personally helped to begin the quest to improve my level of discipleship was the immersion into Church education to learn as much as I could about Church history, the Teaching of the Church, along with reading and studying the Bible. In St. Peter's first Epistle he stated, *"Always be ready to give an explanation to anyone who asks you for a reason for your hope."*[56] That experience in the car years earlier, where I was unable to answer questions about my faith, finally raised my Faith consciousness that I was sorely lacking in that area.

---

[56] 1 Peter 3:15

The improved command of my Faith and Church Teaching at least gave me a firm base ground to grow my discipleship. Not that one needs to be a Bible scholar to be a disciple of Christ. Just look at the Apostles. They did not even have a Bible to show them the way. Knowledge of one's Faith is important though. One cannot emulate and teach what one does not know and believe. I love listening to Catholic Radio. The Catholic Answers Live radio show on EWTN equips one with a full base of apologetic question responses that Catholics frequently field from Protestants, non-believers, and other Catholics as well.

The ultimate challenge now presented: how to implement the book learning and apologetic knowledge to act and serve as an intentional disciple; to take the Word of God to the masses, to be a missionary. Being focused to learn and feel comfortable to discuss the Bible is a good step, but now need to step out and to put that learning into action. As Pope Francis challenges, he does not want his parishioners and clergy to lock themselves in their churches singing Alleluias all their lives. He wants all to get out into the world, into the community to spread God's Word; to energize the Church and the world around; to be an intentional disciple and to make new intentional disciples along the way.

With my involvement in other ministries, such as Boy Scouts, Vocations Awareness, Teen Religious Ed and retreat programs, Discipleship committee, Extraordinary Minister of the Eucharist, and Knights of Columbus, I have an opportunity to now use my Christian education and Faith gained to sow seeds and witness to these communities – and sometimes use words.

Now, given the entry level of my current discipleship involvement, my next challenge is, how can I improve and become a better disciple? How can I better bring the Word of God out to my societies I live in and interacted with? How can I be a better disciple and sow seeds to grow other disciples? Do I need to get involved with more ministries, or do I need to do the ministries I currently partake in better? I'll tell you what, I will just ask Jesus and see what He has to say. I may just write a book.

> *I pray that all my readers be inspired to know Jesus better, to hear God's calling to be His disciple to spread His Word to the world; to use God's gifts to their highest levels in order to do God's will and spread His love and His Church to the world; to be part of God's prayer for the salvation of the world. Amen.*

# Chapter 14: New Appreciation Of The Beatitudes

Due to my fire experience, the Beatitude verses, found in Matthew and Luke, burst into life for the first time. I had never had a personal reference point to really understand and appreciate what Jesus was talking about when presenting the Beatitudes to the crowds of followers that heard His teaching that day. There were eight "Blesseds" identified between Matthew's passage (Matthew 5:1-12), the Sermon on the Mount, and Luke's passage (Luke 6:20-23), the Sermon on the Plain, where Jesus taught His Beatitudes to His followers. The eight Blesseds were:

Poor/poor in spirit, they who mourn, the meek, the hungry/hunger and thirsty for righteousness, the merciful, clean of heart, peacemakers, and the hated/persecuted.

So how do these line up with how we live our lives? Jesus basically says that these are the attributes where one really is able to experience the fullness of His love, mercy and peace. What do the Beatitudes really mean? What challenge do they really pose in order to attain peace and the Lord's Salvation?

If one had approached me to define how I measured up with Jesus' challenges prior to the fire, I would have given a different perspective of the Beatitudes than I have now. I would have told you as long as one is living a "good and clean life" you pretty much fit in with what the Beatitudes are asking for. Being a good person means:

- Since I am not extravagant and there are many other people that have much more money and able to buy more and fancier possessions than I have, I then fit the Blessed are the poor Beatitude.

- I am not happy all the time and a few bad things have happened to me so I guess I fit in with the Blessed are those who mourn.

- The meek? Well, I am not too overbearing. I am not pushy as are other people I know so I guess I can check that one off as well.

- I watch my food dollars and sometimes I miss a meal or two so check on the Blessed are the hungry and thirsty.

- Merciful? I say, "thank you" and help people out when I can, so I can mark off Blessed are the merciful as well.

- Clean of heart? I follow the 10 Commandments most of the time. I mostly watch all G and PG rated movies. That is pretty clean of heart.

- I hate conflict and at least look the other way so do not make things worse. Check on Blessed are the peacemakers.

- Every once in a while, people yell at me for no reason or make fun of me, so at times I feel persecuted.

I felt pretty righteous. I was a good person. I, in part, did everything on the Beatitude list. I thought that was what the Beatitudes were all about. I felt pretty good about myself. I had successfully played the Beatitudes game. I was assured of the Lord's love, peace and Salvation – right?

I should have known. Jesus never made a simple easy check list in His life. Living a true Beatific life style will prove to actually be really tough, almost an impossible task.

> *"Then many of his disciples who were listening said, 'This saying is hard; who can accept it?' Since Jesus knew that his disciples were murmuring about this, he said to them, "Does this shock you?"*[57]

I discovered I was taking the minimalist road to Salvation. "What is the least I need to do to be assured of my place in Heaven?" After experiencing the peace of losing my possessions, I realized that the

---

[57] John 6:60-61

peace I felt in prior times, being a "good person", was far short of what I felt during and after the fire. I was definitely selling myself short all that time when I played the minimalist Beatitude game. There was something much better out there for me. I just needed a little shove from the Almighty to see God's true way he wanted me to live in order to garner His true Kingdom, His true rewards.

Many people get trapped in the minimalist mode thinking God surely would not deny them Heaven if I just live a "good and clean life, for instance, like the one I happen to be living now?" Why should I change? I am living a good life. In John 14:2, Jesus says, *"In My Father's house there are many dwelling places."* What kind of dwelling will Jesus prepare for you? Will a person living only as a "Good Person" be invited into God's house? The following verses seem to speak to a person wanting to only live a good and clean life. One that is willing to be good but not too good. One that holds God at arm's length, choosing to pick and choose and define for one's self what "being a good person" means.

> *"I know your works; I know that you are neither cold nor hot. I wish you were either cold or hot. So, because you are lukewarm, neither hot nor cold, I will spit you out of my mouth."*[58]

> *"Then they will answer and say, 'Lord, when did we see you hungry or thirsty or a stranger or naked or ill or in prison, and not minister to your needs?' He will answer them, 'Amen, I say to you, what you did not do for one of these least ones, you did not do for me.' And these will go off to eternal punishment, but the righteous to eternal life."*[59]

After losing all possessions, I realized the difference between lukewarm and being a "good person". They are actually one and the same. A "good person" strives to do nothing to injure or create ill will,

---

[58] Revelation 3:15-16
[59] Matthew 25:44-46

to cause controversy, to go out of one's way to make no waves. A "good person" looks the other way to justify walking away from an uncomfortable encounter with a person in need – another words, lukewarm. The question a "Good Person" must answer is, "Have I accepted Jesus into my heart, or am I just emulating what I think 'good' looks and feels like?"

To be a "hot" Christian, I discovered I needed to be and act a lot differently. I needed to deviate from being an "invisible Catholic" to step boldly out to become an active and intentional disciple serving my fellow brothers, sisters and my Lord – to risk losing everything to gain everything from God.

Jesus, as one of my gifts received from the fire, showed me what it was like to be poor. He just showed me one of the eight Blesseds. When I walked out of that burning house, I had nothing. I left all my possessions behind to burn and smolder away. As stated earlier in the book, while I watched everything that I owned, everything that I earned money to buy, vanish in front of my eyes, the weight of those possessions seemed to float up as the smoke of the burning blaze across the street from where I stood watching my home being consumed. I felt the grasp, that each one of those things had on me, let go as they burned to a crisp. My stuff distraction was erased, leaving behind the Lord's Beatific peace.

For a period of about one week, my family and I were poor. Everything from the point of the fire itself until we moved into our temporary housing, everything we wore, ate, drank or lived in was provided by the generosity of another person. We had and owned nothing.

For the first time, I realized what the Beatitudes meant and what sacrifice it took to satisfy just one of those eight. Even though I had nothing, I would argue that the week period after the fire was the most joyful and peaceful week of my life. Was there anxiety? Yes, there was. For my family's sake I needed to start the process of putting our lives back together. And, oh yes, there was the stress of the insurance process that had to play out as well. Added to that was the uncertainty of what the future would bring with all the new conditions imposed by the fire. But even with those added worries, they seemed insignificant, surmountable. The joy and peace I felt not only outweighed those worries, it drowned the worries completely out. They did not matter, and joy and peace prevailed.

In spite of a mammoth task ahead and the uncertain future, I, for the first time, felt truly free. I had no possessions to hold me down anymore. I could concentrate on God's will and God's plan for me. The level of joy that I experienced after the phenomenon of losing all possessions was totally counter intuitive to me – and as mentioned during the fire chapter, counter intuitive to the rest of the neighborhood as well. The world has taught us to equate happiness with wealth. The more wealth and possessions you own, the happier one should be, right? My experience after the fire definitely proved that theory wrong where I had no possessions yet experienced the happiest and most peaceful week of my life.

The experience that I was blessed to have been given by God showed me that to truly be poor, one must have total detachment from worldly goods. To experience true peace, one must be stripped down to his/her essence with no other distractions of and from the world. Being poor does not just mean that you do not have as many or valued possessions or less money as some other person. It is a gut wrenching challenge. It is not a soft "do the best you can" challenge. We are talking about a life changing and total mindset reversing event. The challenge Jesus gave to the young rich man. The challenge the rich man could not perform *"because he had many possessions"*.[60]

Jesus is not asking us to just be good. He is challenging us to revolutionize our lives; to eliminate attachments to our "gods" that we hold before Him. Be ready to give it all up and all away if and when He asks you to, without hesitation. To willingly and unconditionally step into the unknown and the frightening to see the face of God.

So, if you desire total peace and the experience of the Lord's total and infinite love, this takes a major leap of courage and Faith. The

---

[60] Mark 10:22

price for total peace and God's love is total detachment from the world and the worlds' influence. The courage and Faith to give it all away. The courage to truly and completely hunger and thirst for Jesus' love and mercy. The courage to boldly proclaim the Word of God and to boldly live one's life as an example of Jesus even though this will bring ridicule from the world.

**Blessed Are The Merciful**

When you assess the list of the Beatitudes, four of them amount to what could be described as "afflictions" (Poor, Mourn, Hungry and Thirsty, and Persecuted). The other four are Beatitudes of action, to address and protect the needs of the afflicted (Meek, Merciful, Clean of Heart, and Peacemakers). The one Beatitude of action that was highlighted specifically during the fire experience was, "Blessed Are the Merciful". The Merriam-Webster dictionary gives two facets of the word, "merciful": 1. Compassionate and 2. Providing relief. Through the fire experience I was fortunate, at that time, to be on both sides of this Beatitude. As soon as I determined that the fire was Jesus' "bad thing to happen", I unconditionally, generously and joyfully provided all I had to the Lord so that His will could be done. Then, being poor, I was the conduit, the subject of the Lord's mercy as my fellow neighbors tended to my family's needs – also with unconditional generosity and joy.

> *"For I was hungry and you gave me food, I was thirsty and you gave me drink, a stranger and you welcomed me, naked and you clothed me, ill and you cared for me, in prison and you visited me."*[61]

So, how is Jesus challenging us and calling us, per His Beatitude teaching, to be merciful? What was Jesus trying to convey to His listeners then and to us today? Again, the Beatitude call to be merciful is not just a "do the best you can to help the afflicted", feel good statement. It is a gut wrenching challenge to divorce one's self from his/her wealth, time and talent to be able to consistently give generously and with joy. We are called to instantaneously respond to

---

[61] Matthew 25:35-36

a need with whatever mercy component that we possess that the recipient is in need of. This is a tough thing for us that "have much" and "have more" gifted to us. There is a worldly tendency to hold on to what you have and not let go. This hoarding tendency acts contrary to mercy. Jesus is asking just the opposite – to be unafraid to give it all away because you will get it back and much more besides in return if you do.

It is that last part, that leap of Faith, that we all struggle with. We humans with our human eyes see everything as a transaction – I give you $1, you give me the widget I purchased. I now have a widget but have $1 less than I had before. In God, transactions are much different. It is very hard for our human brains to wrap our heads around God's version, His Godly promised transaction – I give the person in need $1 and at the end, not only do I not have $1 less, but get 100 or even more measures worth of blessings (and sometimes those include worldly valued blessings as well) in return.

Through this passage in Matthew, as stated above, Jesus commands us to share in another's Beatitude moments and challenges. By providing aid and sharing our wealth (physical as well as time and talents) with those in need, we become participants in the Beatific peace and joy available to the afflicted person(s). Our propensity to give up of our wealth and possessions, to come to the aid of those in need, demonstrates to God the extent of the grip which our wealth and possessions has or does not have on us. When sharing our wealth and other gifts, we not only give the physical assistance needed, but we actually add to the peace and joy of the person afflicted by lessening his/her burdens; allowing them to see God more clearly through their suffering as some of those burdens are eased by a Good Samaritan effort. We, through that act of mercy given, gain immense grace, joy and peace received back in return for our act of love shared.

Wealth is not in itself intrinsically bad. In the Book of Matthew; however, Jesus states, *"It is easier for a camel to pass through the eye of a needle than for one who is rich to enter the kingdom of God.*"[62] If we learn to be generous with our possessions, money, time and talents, we lessen the degree that our wealth enslaves us (per the question raised earlier, "Does my wealth serve God or me?"). As we are cheerfully and unconditionally able to part with our wealth, Jesus no longer sees us chained and shackled to our worldly wealth, but blesses us in growth of spiritual wealth instead – and frequently we find that we are blessed in other ways as well.

The people that came to our aid after the fire exhibited the Lord's generosity by sharing their wealth – money, time, talent and possessions. When people came to our aid, those weeks after the fire, there was no hesitation in their hearts to share their wealth with us. After all, their wealth was not theirs but that given to them by God, so were actually sharing what was God's anyway. The thing that excited me most, was seeing the joy each person, coming to our aid, exhibited; the joy received by this encounter with me, a poor person in need. Their joy beamed from their eyes. Their whole bodies were filled with joy as they shared their item of generosity. When they walked away, I could feel and visibly see the elevation of their grace they had just received from Jesus and the Holy Spirit.

Their generosity saved my family and me. By reducing our burdens, induced by our dire situation after the fire, my community pulled us up from the abyss and allowed me to view and take an active role in God's plan in action. Without the unconditional and generous acts of kindness and mercy extended, I am sure that my vision of what was happening to us would have been severely clouded. I would have been swept up by the tragedy and not seen the hand of God in action. By coming to my aid, my benefactors reduced my burdens with their charity, to not only give me the sight of my Lord, but also allowed the immense outpouring of love and good works that Jesus had put into place to energize the world around us.

The question that I had then, of which the Lord did not give me vision to, is any long lasting effect that the fire experience had on any

---

[62] Matthew 19:24

one of the people engaged during those weeks after the fire. I only wonder if, by the charity shared with us, that the act, perhaps, inspired other modes of service given to other ministries, such as disaster relief or homeless efforts. Perhaps other new ministries were established based on the grace and joy felt by one's saying "Yes" to the Lord on this initial endeavor. Perhaps the person now is more disposed to generosity and unconditionally acts on needs of mercy as they come along. I would feel so blessed if someone's interaction with my need for mercy (the seed) cultivated into a lovely flower of further service to others in need.

What Jesus is really asking and mandating, is that we develop a virtue of habitual charity, the habitual act of sharing of one's wealth, time and talents with those in need or those in the throes of a Beatific affliction event. When acting as a habitual charitable Christian, we achieve not a temporary, one-time grace gained from individual charitable act(s), but a long lasting, lifelong experience by grace, of Beatific peace and joy, gained by a virtue cultivated of committing of one's self to do works of mercy. When one no longer has to contemplate the cost of an act of mercy; when one just acts as the need is witnessed, the more complete and long lasting the Beatific peace and joy remains. Jesus' challenge from the quote above calls us to habitually and unconditionally share our wealth. We are called to sever our attraction and grip on our wealth, and use our wealth and talents, that God has so lavishly given us, to lessen burdens and bring others to Christ.

As can be seen by the above two situations – the wealthy and the needy – both can be shackled by their individual conditions and situations needing to be freed to enjoy Jesus' peace and joy. The needy person, in the throes of a Beatific situation, may be embroiled and buried by the tragedy or condition that one is in, seeing no way out. One cannot see out of the forest and misses the opportunity to experience the graces and Jesus' outstretched arms awaiting them. On the other hand, a wealthy person is trapped and shackled by the greed to hold on tight to his/her wealth; unwilling to let loose of their wealth that God has so graciously given; wealth that was undeserved but given anyway.

Note: One does not have to be Donald Trump rich to have a deep attraction problem with their possessions. I have seen homeless people go to war to prevent losing one of their prized possessions. The homeless person's stuff can also shackle one to their pile or cart just as much as a Billionaire can be shackled to his/her stock portfolio. In this instance, the homeless person cannot tear him/herself away for a second from one's little pile of possessions without risk of another local looting his/her stash. One can now see, even a homeless person, can be "rich", become shackled, like the monkey with his hand stuck in the milk bottle, to their possessions.

Thus, these two groups – the needy and wealthy – are intertwined and dependent on each other for their salvation. The needy have abundant graces available to them due to their sufferings experienced. The wealthy have the means to share their wealth, to care for the needy, to ease their suffering. This sharing of resources will give people in need a better vantage angle to view God in their lives; to take full advantage of their Beatific graces. The wealthy, at the same time, gain Jesus' love and peace as they are first freed from the shackles of the wealth shared with the needy. The rich person is able to share in the needy person's Beatific peace and joy as well. When the two combine, the world becomes Godlier as both the needy and wealthy attain an abundance of Jesus, Jesus' love, mercy and joy, in their hearts.

As presented in the prior discussion about discipleship, when people exhibit the Lord's call to unconditionally give and receive mercy, that act breeds more acts of mercy as others witness and accept Jesus' challenge to give and receive mercy unconditionally. This Good Samaritan ripple effect could then change the world.

If one is currently embroiled in the throes of his/her own Beatific event, I pray that you are able to look toward Jesus and know that He loves you infinitely. I pray that you have the vision to feel Jesus' outstretched arms and the blessings and graces He is heaping on you to sooth your suffering. The beckoning of the world sees Beatific suffering as loss only, with no chance of good from it. I pray that, as I was able to do during the weeks after the fire, that you are able to see Jesus in all your surroundings and gain Beatific peace and joy by lovingly carrying your cross. I also pray, again as my family experienced in our tragedy, that grace filled benefactors will come to your aid to lift your spirits and remove any shackles from the world that prevent you from enjoying your deserved Beatific peace, love and joy. To be able to endure Beatific suffering with peace and joy becomes the essence of sainthood.

> *Lord I pray that you send your Holy Spirit to enter the lives of the readers of this book to give an insight of the way to radically change their lives per Your will to make them inspired, intentional and habitual Beatific disciple Christians. Amen.*

## Chapter 15: Go Tell It On The Mountain!

> *"It is impossible for us not to speak about what we have seen and heard."*[63]
>
> *"And [immediately] the man's ears were opened, his speech impediment was removed, and he spoke plainly. He ordered them not to tell anyone. But the more he ordered them not to, the more they proclaimed it."*[64]

When you have been touched by the Lord, how can you keep from singing? Immediately, as the fire story started to develop on the morning of July 5, I knew this story, unfolding in front of me, was one that had to be told. I guess why now vs. writing the story right after the fire when it was a fresh experience? I guess I had to warm up to it a little and make sure that, as far as I could see, God's plan had a chance to play out. I had to take some time to get a fuller understanding and grasp the vast phenomenon that God had propagated through my family. During the weeks of the fire experience, it seemed that I was playing the role of a news reporter documenting the story for a future article. So possibly this book is part of God's plan as well.

As previously mentioned, right after the fire, I was looking for somewhere, some audience to tell the story to. It was so magnificent, so Spiritual that it begged to be told. My only concern was, who would believe me? God coming to visit with me to prepare me for this tragedy? The fact that I was joyous when watching my worldly possessions go up in smoke? That sounds like a tall tale that might be hard to find an accepting audience to appreciate.

My first chance to tell the fire story materialized when I accepted a second chance to join a CRHP retreat formation team. The formation group for the 1997 Spring session only had 4 people that volunteered

---

[63] Acts 4:20. Peter's statement after he and John were warned by the Sanhedrin not to preach about Jesus any more.
[64] Mark 7:35-36 Jesus cures a deaf man.

## I Have Come To Set The Earth On Fire

to continue on for the formation team and would need at least one more to effectively put on that next retreat. I talked to the CRHP director at St Lawrence and submitted my request to volunteer for the formation team. I told him that our fire experience was so Spiritually enlightening that I needed to give my talk at the CRHP retreat. He agreed. And I was now a 2nd time CRHP presenter participant.

During the formation process, came the task to put together the talk I was to give. Surely, with the recentness and being such a moving experience, the talk should be easy, a breeze to write. I started writing my script and the words just did not come. I was frustrated because this should be an easy no brainer. I agonized for weeks and what I had put down just was not feeling right. I finally completed the talk script but again I was not comfortable with what I had prepared. It was now within a week prior to the retreat. What I had completed still did not feel like the talk that should be given. I started to get a little nervous. I was under a bit of pressure. Time was getting short. I was to convey a major experience with the Almighty Lord and what I had on paper to date fell well short of the speech needed to properly proclaim the glorious events that God had put together through my family and me.

Well, I guess the Holy Spirit also had the same concern. Early Tuesday morning, during the week leading up to the talk, I was in a deep sleep. Suddenly, I woke up about 2:00am (which coincidentally was the same time I was awakened the morning of the fire) and instantly, the words for my talk were running in my head. This was the talk that Jesus wanted me to give. I was compelled to get up and head to the computer and after a couple of hours, the first fire talk was ready to give. It was as if the Holy Spirit was dictating the script as I was typing away. I must say, the Holy Spirit is a much better speechwriter than I am. It seems that I was trying to write my words instead of what the Lord wanted me to say. It has been His show all along, so I am glad to have finally got it right in the end.

The day of the retreat came. I had conceived a grand plan for a good theatrical element in the beginning of my talk to set the stage for the fire talk. I should have known the "My Plan" part was doomed from the beginning. I wore the clothes (shorts and t-shirt) that I had on when I escaped the fire that morning. Over the shorts I wore a pair of sweatpants. My plan was to start the talk then remove my shoes, glasses and the sweats to reveal my fire day outfit. When I did so, unfortunately, I had forgotten to zip up and my fly in my shorts was open. That was a bit embarrassing, but I guess a little comedic relief at the start is good for the talk.

The first fire speech's audience was riveted as I went through basically the same fire story as has been captured in this book earlier. The shorts and t-shirt really helped drive home the concept of how desperate, homeless and poor our situation was at that moment of July 5, 1996 - possessed only the clothes on our backs. CRHP turned out to be a great place to give the first fire talk. It felt good to give the speech. The speech that the Holy Spirit dictated to me flowed out like honey. Since the retreat participants were all from St Lawrence parish, all pretty much knew about our story, so I just needed to fill in the blanks and tie things together for them to make the Lord's points. Since some of the participants were ones who gave us assistance, it was another chance for me to thank them for their generosity. I am hoping I encouraged them and challenged them to continue to find ways to be better stewards with their wealth and possessions.

What now? The first volley of the fire story was shot to the ten CRHP retreat participants and the four CRHP teammates. I knew the story was not to stop there. As the weeks after the fire went on and God's plan unfolded, I mentioned to myself that this is a great story that needs to be written down. I guess I had to wait until the time was right. As the years went by, the fire story was etched into my brain and begged to come out, but remained unwritten. Probably for the same reason that I had so much trouble writing my original script. I was not ready Spiritually. I did not have a good enough understanding of my Faith, so I did not have a clear enough understanding of some of the events that happened and for what purpose they happened.

The second occasion for the fire speech was a talk given at our current parish of Our Lady of Angles in Allen, TX about 11 years after the fire. My family had moved down to Plano, TX in 1998 as I took a new job in the Dallas area. So now, the fire story was about to travel from Indianapolis to our new parish, Our Lady of Angels in Allen Texas.

It was first amazing how God inserted me into the Parish Council meeting, where one of the meeting agenda items on their docket just happened to be, finding speaker options to speak at the next parish Sunday luncheon presentation where the topic of the talk would be, "Why do bad things happen to good people". The parish had established a monthly Sunday afternoon luncheon talk series where at each session, one of the parishioners gave a talk on whatever topic was chosen for the meeting. I just happened to be at this PPC meeting to pitch their support for our new Boy Scout troop that a group of parishioners and I were trying to form. Low and behold, I was there. When the agenda item came up to discuss who might the PPC find to give that month's talk, I told a bit of the fire story and pointed out that a possible angle, that the person's talk could take, could be related to suffering in conjunction with carrying out God's plan of Salvation. After they heard a little of my story I was then unanimously asked to give my speech. I really did not intend that little pitch to be an audition for the part. I said one of my *"help!"* prayers to Jesus and He said, *"you're in"*. So, I agreed. God works in mysterious ways.

This event that I was speaking at was the first of these presentations that I actually attended personally. I went through a similar problem writing this speech as when writing the CRHP speech. This time, two days before my talk, the Holy Spirit came through again and I finalized my script. This time, I was not as concerned as time drew near to the talk because I knew the Holy Spirit would give me the words – He just waited a little longer this time. I think He was afraid that if He gave me the words too early, I would forget them.

So, the day came for Fire speech #2. I made sure all my wardrobe was in correct attire this time. I did not try the same entrance as before. Besides, I could not even fit into the shorts from the fire (although I still had that pair in my drawer) because my waistline had expanded a bit since.

I did not know beforehand how many people to expect for the talk session so was surprised when there were at least 50 people there. I was Spirit filled again as the talk was given. I am not a gifted speaker by any stretch of imagination, but charged through the talk. I was amazed looking into the audience at the intent look on everyone's face. I felt like a fine orator. I was worried that my audience would be bored, or the topic would not resonate with them. I could not have been more wrong. It was impressive that that many people sat so still and quiet for the 30-minute talk and were so intensely listening to something that I had to say. It had to be the Holy Spirit, He was really giving the talk anyway. Words came out again like honey. As happened during the weeks after the fire, it was my gums flapping but the Holy Spirit was doing the talking.

At one part early in the talk, I really touched a chord with the crowd. I had just made the point that the fire, being such a monumental event in our family's lives, became a date place marker that family time was understood – before and after fire. I saw a number of heads bob up and down in approval. After the talk several came over and commented about their own momentous occasion in their lives where their same time place marker was put in place – time before and after. Some of these occasions were related to a spouse passing away. Some had other equally traumatic events that had happened such as a bad car accident. It was as if we were all in the same club together.

I do not know how many lives were touched by fire speech #2, but I am guessing a little over 50. The story is still resonating to this day with some of the parishioners in attendance that day. Again, I had a chance to be Jesus' disciple and hopefully gave hope to those in need that day. I am betting a number of participants may have had, since the speech, their own traumatic event. Hopefully memories from this speech stayed with them and gave hope of the good that was done, the hope that their event would eventually play itself out, and would be rewarded by God for their adversity. Who knows, maybe the talk inspired others to write down or give their own speech of how God acted in their lives through their adversity.

So, time again passed after the second speech. I continued to feel the tug from God to write His fire story. I was always too busy, traveled too much or just did not feel the inspiration of the Spirit talking to me yet. Perhaps I needed to spruce up my catechesis a bit. I started listening to Catholic Radio after Guadalupe Radio Station started to broadcast in the Dallas area. I listened to shows such as Catholic Answers Live (highly recommended to all) which is a call in question and answer apologetics radio show. I learned a lot about my Faith which even challenged a few practices of my own that I never considered might not be in total compliance with Church teaching. This snippet of knowledge introduced me to books on Catholicism where even more was learned. I started volunteering to teach Religious Ed in Ryan's classes which I not only learned from but challenged me to make sure I was practicing what I taught.

I followed Ryan all the way from $5^{th}$ grade up through high school in the OLA Religious Ed program. As the kids got older, their questions also became more profound and difficult to answer. I found myself having to study even more to keep up with the questions I was fielding.

My life was really rocked when Ryan went into the high school program. The Teen Director of Religious Education was a Spirit filled dynamo, Matt Decker. I had never seen anyone with his zeal for Christ. He took a program that was lackluster and transformed it into full blown Spirit filled discipleship fest occasions. He had teens on fire for the Lord. It was great to see their faces when Matt would walk into the room. The Spirit level would dial up a few notches right there. The look in his eyes was so exciting. You could see his enthusiasm for the Lord. He truly was a Lord's disciple.

I was able to participate in several teen retreats where the older teens actually put the retreat together and gave the talks. The adults were just there to keep the schedule going. It was so wonderful watching the older teens give their young faith stories during their talks. On occasions, their passion for Christ moved me to tears. If we can keep these teens energized for Christ as they were, we are turning the world over to some very capable hands for the Church's future. As a product of this discipleship based Religious Ed program, one of the boys in Ryan's class, as stated earlier, was so moved that he decided he had a calling from God to enter the Seminary. He is now in his first year in Seminary continuing his discernment for his Priestly Vocation.

My Spiritual development and learning over these years helped form me to finally write this book. However, it took another jolt to get me off my dead horse to get started. I guess the Lord felt I did not have enough free time, so in March of this year, the company I worked for laid me off from my job. Now I had all the time I wanted to write the Lord's fire book. As weeks went by, I felt the tug even more to get started. Then the final push. When talking to an Our Lady of Angels parishioner at church one day, she, out of the blue, asked me if I was the one who gave the speech about why bad things happen to good people. I was taken back that after 10 years the speech was still fresh enough in someone's mind to even remember the topic let alone that I was the one that gave it. That was the final push. That night I started working to establish the chapters and structure the book would consist of. That was the start and what you are now reading is the fruits.

It has been a long road to get to the point to finally put these words on paper. I sincerely hope that my readers are half as riveted as my prior two audiences have been. I offer the challenge back to you now as well. If you have a story of a monumental and Spiritual event or journey in your or your family's life, go ahead and write it down. Even if you never publish your work it will bear fruits. I remember reading a story that my grandmother Chomistek wrote about the days of and after my grandfather was involved in a major gas refinery explosion in the early 1950's. She documented her feelings and what happened over the days at the hospital leading up to his death. It was such a great slice of life and family history documentation. I was mesmerized by the story as I read it. Especially documenting events of a grandfather that I had never met.

Just writing this book was a very enlightening thing. Reliving these stupendous happenings and the people involved often brought me to tears more than once as I was typing the words. Also, the Holy Spirit blessed me with several revelations about sections as I was writing them. Several instances, after I wrote to report a fact of something that happened, the situation tugged at me that there was another meaning or reason for what and why it happened. Maybe that day or a week later, something I saw or read would all of a sudden click. It may have just popped into my head, put there by the Holy Spirit. Regardless, things that I did not understand but documented instantly became clear. Again, I recommend to my readers to start to document your story. I am betting that you will have the same emotional and wondrous time writing your story as I did. Go tell it on the mountain!

*Lord, send down your Spirit to my readers so they can boldly proclaim your name and deeds and renew the face of the earth. Amen.*

## Chapter 16: God's Most Precious Gift – My Family

I always loved my family very much prior to the fire, but sometimes you do not really know how much one takes one's family for granted until a situation arises where the real possibility to lose family member(s) happens. That point of realization happened to me during the fire. The first walk through of the house that morning smacked me in the face how close we all came to lose each other that early morning of July 5th. The chills I received, contemplating what could have happened, brought reality and an all new appreciation of the wonderful gift that the Lord had given me and had then re-given me again that morning.

The first time I really contemplated the possibility of losing my family started with the onset of the pre fire "something bad to happen" prophecies. When the messages were received, one of my first questions back to the Lord asked if the "bad thing" would involve the loss of one or more of my family members. That was as bad as I could contemplate. God did answer back that all family would be unhurt and uninjured. I continued to ask God the question, though, about my family's safety, for about a week, then I finally felt comfortable and at peace that the promise really did come from God rather than something that I fabricated in my own mind – wanting it to be true. Even during the period where I was not entirely sure if the promise of my family's safety came from God, I still received the deep cleansing feeling of peace when the prayer session ended. Once I was sure the promise did validly come from God, a new level of peace was felt to each successive prayer discussion with the Lord.

Starting with the prophecies, I really began to fully appreciate the awesome gift God had bestowed on me with the gift of my wife and kids. After we all exited safely from the house that morning, and I realized the fire was the bad thing foretold, I was deeply relieved and intensely thankful that the Lord's promises had come true and all were safe.

A major revelation obtained from the fire experience was, human life, and especially that of my family members, was the most precious gift that God could have possibly given to the human race. As I watched my house and possessions be consumed by the flames, I was totally OK with the reality of losing all my possessions. Possessions have a finite value due to their manmade origins. Once it was a foregone conclusion that all was lost, I was at total peace with that fact. The reason I was totally at peace with the loss of my possessions was that my family was in complete safety and unhurt. My family, with infinite value, due to their divine origin and divine gift, given to me by God to care and protect. That early morning, I felt like the richest man on earth, even though at that time the only things owned were the clothes on my back. I had, though, the most precious of possessions, gifts that were bestowed directly by God – my family and my family's love and support!

At that point, I was keenly aware that the possessions being consumed could be replaced. It would take a while and we would have to deal with the insurance company to get our claims paid, but in the end all lost could and was replaceable. On the other hand, I came minutes away from potentially losing possibly all my family members, or at least seeing them injured. I became keenly aware that a lost family member could not be replaced. I realized how blessed I was; how loved I was by the Father that he spared my family, even to the extent of no injuries.

Later in that first day when we were able to go back into the house to see the damage, we again got a good look at just how in danger we all were and how blessed we were that God's plan included saving our family. Seeing the charred remains of the upstairs and the heavy debris, that fell on top of the beds where we all slept, was sobering. Considering we were awakened prior to the smoke alarms sounding, the realization that in order for the smoke alarms to sound, the fire had to first break through the walls where we were all sleeping, we felt most fortunate to have escaped before real danger presented itself.

The sequential circumstances that were put into place to wake us up was a miracle. It was a "Big Bang" moment. Just as the universe was created Divinely from nothing to be initiated by the Big Bang, so we were also awakened by means of Divine intervention.

When one comes that close to death and death of family member(s), it forces a new outlook on life; how precious and wonderful such a supreme gift one's family really is. This situation now poses the question, "What are you prepared to lose?" If God was to take something away from you, what would be so valuable to you that you would say without hesitation, "Take anything Lord except for…" After the fire event, there would be no hesitation on my part to say, "Lord you can take anything but please do not take any of my family members."

My family is really the only thing that came naturally and directly from God. All I have comes from God, but my physical possessions came as result of my free will decisions how I spent my wealth that was given by God. My family was a direct gift, directly and naturally from God. I did not have to buy them, invest to save to buy them or hop in the car to drive to the store to get them. Through the grace of God, we became pregnant and there they were, son and daughters, gifts from the Almighty Creator.

Life is so special and wonderful. That first morning was so magnificent watching the sun start to rise. Start to rise on a new day that I could sniff the air. I could look up to the beautiful blue sky. I could rejoice because I was alive, alive by the good graces of our Lord. I was even more thankful because I could walk over and hug and kiss my wife and each one of my kids. That was a glorious day!

I never saw hugging and kissing my family members as a luxury thing. It was one endeavor that I took for granted because I never did see a possible interruption to the being of my family members. I always envisioned my family as always there, a constant. After that first day of the fire, my world was shaken a bit. I felt the mortality of first my family members, then myself. It was a **H**umbling experience. It was also one that exploded my love and appreciation of my family members to a new level. They were truly the most valuable and precious gifts that God had ever given me. A loss of one of my family members would be a true tragedy that could not be put back together as it was before. There would be always a sad void. Not that the Lord would not allow healing and additional graces, but that member would never again be available for a hug, a kiss or a kind word.

But even my children, being gifts from God, are just that. My kids, as well as my wife and I, are but gifts from God to the world. We do not own ourselves. Cathy and I do not or cannot claim ownership of our children. We are all God's "property". Property given to us and the world to be used for God's will and to fulfill God's plan for humanity. Even the gifts of my children are subject to be recalled by the Lord to fulfill His will if He so deems necessary. That is why I am so grateful that the Lord did spare my family and me from the fire. It also validates that, by being saved, all in my family still have a role or mission to play in God's plan for salvation.

Now, the next wonderful gift received as a result of the fire was the birth of our son Ryan. God is so great! Not only did He spare any harm to my existing family members, but he added one more on top of that. As most pregnancies are, but especially this one, Ryan's birth, was a complete surprise. One that we did not ask for but were given out of God's love for us. He knew what we needed and gave. Here we thought that our family with three kids was perfect. God made it even more perfect with number four. Our lives changed again that 9th month after the fire. We all had new roles to play. The three kids were now new older brother and sisters. They acquired a whole new perspective on family life and how a family sticks and works together.

One does not have a chance to test the real mettle of the oneness of a family until it is severely tested by something, *"In this you rejoice, although now for a little while you may have to suffer through various trials, so that the genuineness of your faith, more precious than gold that is perishable even though tested by fire, may prove to be for praise, glory, and honor at the revelation of Jesus Christ"*[65]. I also was

---

[65] 1 Peter 1:6-7

blessed to see how a family such as ours sticks together and handles adversity. I was able to see how the essence of a family extends God's love and each other's determination to get through something as difficult as losing one's home and possessions.

I was so proud of Cathy and the kids. I could see Jesus plus our guardian angels working together to get us through. We were so strong for each other. This situation was new territory for all of us. There was no manual to follow with step by step directions how to recover from such a tragic occurrence. We were there for each over. Cathy and the kids were my strength. We were each other's strength as well.

I never saw fear in any of my family members' faces throughout the ordeal. I never saw despair in their faces either. We knew we would make it through as a family. We knew that whatever the end of the story was, we would write that story as a family. I gained so much strength and power from my family members that I never really was concerned for our future. I was definitely unsure as to what needed to be done or what was to become of us because this was totally new ground. I was always sure that whatever happened, it would be good because we would be together as a family and from what I learned that day of the fire, being together as a family is as good as it gets!

*May the blessings of the Holy Family, Jesus, Mary and Joseph be on each one of my readers that your family stays together and is strong for each other in the good times and the bad and magnifies the face and love of Jesus in all you do and to everyone who comes in contact with you and your family. Amen.*

# I Have Come To Set The Earth On Fire

# Part 3 Closing Thoughts

This section provides the final thoughts summarizing the fire experience and how it affected life afterwards for my family and me. God truly spared us and set my family up to glorify God for all days to come. My family's work is not done yet. We were spared for a reason. God's overall plan is still being written not only for my family and me, but also for you and your family as well.

Part 3 Chapters

Chapter 17: Jesus Is Relentless. He Wants Us All With Him In Heaven.

Chapter 18: Review Of Things Learned From The Fire Experience

1. Put a smoke alarm in the garage
2. Learning Opportunity
3. God is involved in our lives every day
4. Every person has Jesus in their hearts
5. Each person makes the world a better place
6. God rewards people who do His will
7. Everyone is part of God's plan
8. Life is Biblical
9. Charity is explosive
10. Be a Beatitudinal person
11. Be careful (prepared) what you ask God for – He may just give it to you
12. Feel free to put yourself out of your comfort zone and share your time, talent and treasure
13. Prayer is powerful

Chapter 19: Final Concluding Thoughts

## Chapter 17: Jesus Is Relentless. He Wants Us All With Him In Heaven.

There is never a point in one's life where one can look up to Jesus and say, *"Lord, I have done it all. I have done everything you asked of me. I can now just coast and wait until you call me from this life because I have completed everything necessary to be worthy of my Heavenly reward."* Does that sound familiar? That is the question that the young rich man proposed to Jesus, *"All of these I have observed. What do I still lack?"*[66] As soon as we feel that we have it all, Jesus tends to challenge back with, *"Well, sell it all and follow me."*

God still gives my family and me plenty of challenges to persevere through. The fire was not an ending, an *"if you do this, then you have completed all that I ask"* moment. It seems that just when life starts to have a sense of "normal", God is not opposed to introduce a little pot stirring (I have come to afflict the comforted). When things are going well, and life seems to be going on autopilot; when I think that this is how life should be: making money, bank account is growing, job is going well, family is in a smooth and calm routine, that is when the Lord allows things to get shaken up a bit and lets me know that He is not done with me yet because I have not yet finished the race.[67] One cannot quit before the finish line. A marathon is not completed and won by stopping after completing only 20 miles because that seems far enough. When I put my life in cruise control, I am doing just that.

Since the fire, I have been laid off three times, including now when writing this book. Each of these three times, Jesus had a message, a lesson that He wanted me to learn and grasp. The second of these times laid off was the experience that I learned the most from thus far. There were points of humility that God was trying to get me to understand in prior such experiences, but for some reason, it took another major jolt for these things to finally sink in.

---

[66] Matthew 19:20
[67] 2 Timothy 4:7

I was laid off in August of 2001. As many of you may remember, the years of 2001 and 2002 were pretty lean years employment wise. When I was first laid off and started to attend outplacement sessions made available to me, the outplacement counselors, after looking at my resume, all said, "With your credentials you should have no problem landing a job right away." Well, that *"right away"* took a year and a half for me to finally land a job.

I learned three big time things over my year and a half's unemployment stint: First, I always believed that I was so good professionally that if a job ended, I could always walk out and find another. I had a "ME" complex. The gift of a good job given to me by God was under appreciated. I ran my job with that mentality. My bravado set my agenda as "if the boss/company did not value my contributions, I would just take my services elsewhere". To cure that false bravado, the Lord put me on the shelf for a year and a half. When the Lord finally let me out of jail so to speak and found my next job, I went into that next position with a whole different, humbler mindset. I thanked the Lord for my new gift and was thankful, praising God, every day until that job ended over 12 years later.

The second thing learned from that exercise was, God is in charge. God has a plan and despite my efforts to make my own personal situation better or it to go away, God had his own plan; His own time and place for my unemployment to start and end. I learned how to give my troubles, whether financial or just the angst of being unemployed – the humbling loss of personal identity – to God. For I could not solve my situation by my own will. I came to realize that the only way my situation could be handled was to put my trust in God that He had a plan for me and I would have to wait until His situation, His place, and His time happened.

Thirdly, the Lord again had to teach me one more time about humility. It seemed the lessons learned from the fire and all the other situational tutorials sent my way still did not sink in. Doesn't this guy ever get it? One easily becomes defined per what job one has. When a person wants to become familiar with you, one of the first question usually asked is, "What do you do?" Not being able to describe yourself as "the Packaging Engineer for XYZ Company" gives one a sense of loss of identity if one does not have a job to describe. Being unemployed was sometimes a clash between my bruised ego vs. God's will. I do not have to tell you that God always won. I had to learn that I was a special creation of God whether I was employed or not. I had to learn patience because I was working in God's time and not mine. Again, friends and family, as during the fire, came to our aid when needed. Even though they were not asked to do so, they came to our aid exactly when we needed them. When I finally became employed, I found that I was indeed in the right place that God was calling me to be. I then had a great and rewarding 12+ years.

During this period of unemployment, another thing gained was a renewed Spirituality. I learned the graces and comfort that I received when attending daily Mass. I had a chance to sit before the Lord and dialogue with Him. I asked Him, "When is this going to end?" "Is today Your time?" I had a chance to lay out to Him my anxieties pertaining to my being without a job for that extended period of time. During that last few months before I finally found a job, added to our dwindling financial concerns, my oldest daughter started college at Texas A&M. Added to my mounting monthly bills, a regular tuition payment was lumped on top of my family's normal financial obligations. The Lord took care of me and gave me comfort. Comfort is not what I was asking for. I was asking for a job. God gave me comfort instead to say, "It is not time yet. Have peace and know that I am with you and will grant your prayer at the right time and place."

I also discovered discipleship. During 2001-2002, there were many people that were in my same boat. The Telecom industry had just collapsed and the areas near me in Plano and Richardson Texas were teaming with Telecom companies that either closed down or cut way back, spewing computer programmers and project managers onto the job market. They were hurting and scared. Somehow through Church I got involved with an email group – an early kind of chat room – with people that were unemployed. Again, most of these people on the distribution list were long timer unemployed individuals as I was. I started hearing their pain and had a very good feeling where they were coming from because I had those same worries and questions. I realized that I had a voice. A voice that Jesus wanted me to use to disciple to these out of work people. These people were my brothers and sisters and I was now a part of their world. I began to email about how powerful prayer was and that prayer was the answer. God would help make sense and give hope to all in prayer; that there was an end to their situation. My emails pointed out to all that they could not resolve their situation strictly on their own and had to give their cares, frustrations and faith to Jesus. Their situation was now in Jesus' hands so that is where they needed to look toward and pray to. I also proposed and suggested attending church and daily church/Mass if their faith denominations made that available.

Through the email communications, I was not sure what my response back was going to be. Would a bunch of people respond that I was a nut? Respond that my simplistic view to let God takeover is doing more harm than good? Actually, to my surprise, I do not remember any backlash comments received. The one that I do remember came after writing how attending daily Mass gave me comfort. I received an email back from a person with an oriental name thanking me for my insight and taking the time to provide these good words. Now I am not sure what faith discipline this person had or even if he had a faith. Through his email though, I felt a bond. I felt that my humble words proposing Christ as the answer to the afflictions we all suffered was heard and taken to heart. That was a good day for sure when one can make a difference in a life, especially one trying to make sense of what is happening to him even though nothing seems to be making sense at the time.

**Lessons Learned From An Unexpected Source**

The scariest thing, though, that the Lord has asked us to endure thus far was the year we moved to Plano, TX. We were just barely settled in our new home and city. At the time, Ryan was 21 months old. One morning he could not walk. He would take a step then crumple to the ground. Ryan had been running since he was 9 months old, so this was definitely an eye catching situation. Something indeed was very wrong. With great concern, we took Ryan to the Pediatrician. He was diagnosed to have suffered a stroke. This was a scary and frustrating situation where Cathy and I stood helpless and unable to help our poor baby son. There was nothing that we could do. There was nothing that the doctors could really do as well. This gave additional humility and a new challenge that God had put in our lap. In the beginning, Cathy and I were not sure whether Ryan's situation was life threatening. The only thing that we could do was to put this in God's hands and ask others for their prayers as well. I remember a conversation I had with the Lord asking, "After giving us this wonderful gift after the fire, is this how it is going to end?"

We ended up at Children's Hospital in Dallas for the week and Ryan did pull through in the end, thank the Lord, with a full recovery. The real learning, though, that God gave us started when Ryan was moved to a room in the oncology wing – with children that had all types and forms of cancer they were battling. There was a flu epidemic going on at the time and all the other rooms were full of flu patients. Since Ryan was not contagious with anything, he ended up in the oncology ward because that was the only place with an open room/bed.

Now that was an experience! I still vividly remember seeing little boys and girls walking around the floor pushing their IV holders with their medicine regimens dripping into their arms. By this time, Ryan was out of the woods and on the road to recovery. I felt a definite mix of feelings during my daily visits to see Ryan. Ryan, the poor kid, had to go through a regimen of blood and other tests the doctors ran to try to identify the origin and severity of his stroke, but we were told by the doctors that he would make a full recovery. I was joyous that my son had been spared just as his family had been during the fire. I was saddened though seeing all these poor boys and girls that most likely were not long for this world. I felt a bit guilty because the parents of these children had a completely different outlook and future planned for their families vs. our own.

Again, the face of Jesus showed up. I did not see sorrow or fear in the eyes and hearts of these young children. Their eyes were alive and glowing. God had showed me again how powerful His love and nurturing grace can be and is. God bless all those children and their parents for showing me the face of Jesus again in their suffering.

So, as can be seen by these examples, the little curve balls that life/God throws us are meant to teach important lessons, not only to us but others as well; to make everyone's faith stronger in Christ. If we do not learn the lessons, God tends to keep giving us teaching moments until they finally sink in. One never stops learning, even though we sometimes think we know it all. We learn, whether we want to or not, because that is Jesus' mandate. We are never done. We have never crossed the finish line until we stand at the pearly gates met by St. Peter.

Sometimes we need to really search for what God is trying to show and teach us. The real teaching may not be related to the initial event at all. It may be a second unexpected teaching that happens as a result - such as the example above form Ryan's stroke.

There were lessons gained while going through Ryan's road to recovery, but what Jesus really wanted me to see was the kids in the cancer ward. Some people tell a story that seems to go around the world before getting to the real point. Well, sometimes God works that way as well. When things happen to you, be patient and be prepared to see and feel God's real calling; His real message to you; His lesson He means for you to learn, and His total and unconditional Love for you.

Again, as experienced during the fire story, one's sufferings can be the learning moment that Jesus has planned and put in place for someone else's benefit; someone else's Faith journey. The kids with cancer and their families had no idea that their walk with Jesus; their glorious battle with life's mortality that week Ryan resided in the oncology ward, was also a lesson that God had meant for me as well.

Jesus wants every one of us to attain our Heavenly Reward and join with Him in Heaven. To do that, we need to be "tested in fire" to get there. Sometimes it is our own fire that tests us. Sometimes it is a fellow brother's fire that leads us to further communion with Jesus our Lord. Lord, I look forward to our next adventure together.

## I Have Come To Set The Earth On Fire

*Lord, give me a soft and warm heart. Let Your teachings be adsorbed by my mind and my heart to do Your will and bring me to Your Salvation. May I also be your relentless witness to others that I may bring other brothers and sisters with me to our Eternal Salvation, to our Heavenly rewards. Amen.*

## Chapter 18: Review Of Things Learned From The Fire Experience

1. **Put a smoke alarm in the garage.** I know this departs from the spiritual flavor of this book but is a definite lesson learned from my experience that needs to be told. Surprisingly I have not seen any new or existing house that has a smoke detector installed in the garage. That is amazing considering all the flammable liquids, flammable things in your garage (cars full of gas and oil, cans of gas, paint, paint thinner, oily rags, lumber etc.) plus possible origins of sparks and flames. In the case of our home that burned, the gas furnace and gas water heater were located in the garage. Also, as was the cause of our fire, there is electrical wiring as well.

    Why would you not want to have a smoke alarm in your garage and also if your garage has an attic, there as well? In our situation, the fire started in the garage. The key strategy for the smoke alarm system is to provide an early warning alert of the fire's origin before the fire progresses to an out of control critical safety stage so occupants can safely get out of the building. The fire at our house was allowed to progress to a much more mature and dangerous level before the smoke alarm system, located within the interior living space of the house, kicked in. If not for God's intervention to wake up my son and wife, our escape from the burning home would have been much more perilous – and maybe by that time impossible. In order for the smoke detectors mounted within our inside rooms to register their alarm warning, the fire had to progress to the point where it broke through the interior walls and/or ceiling of the house. By that time, it was raging well out of control and potentially could have blocked my family's pathway to safety, trapping us in our upstairs bedrooms.

    Ever since the fire, I have recommended garage smoke detectors to anyone I know that is building a home. My current home now has a smoke detector located in the garage. Be safe, put a smoke detector in your garage if you do not have one already!

2. **Learning Opportunity:** Bad things happen all the time. What defines the difference between a tragedy and a life changing event? The difference between the two comes down to what was learned or not learned. A bad decision or event becomes a tragedy when nothing is learned. If one continues with life unchanged as before, such as the mindset, "that was just an isolated event", allows the person to crawl under a rock and miss an opportunity to improve. This would be again an example of the *"useless servant"* in Matthew's story of the Parable of the Talents. The servant given 1 talent buries it, afraid that he will lose it, but in the end, loses everything because the servant failed to be a good steward of his charge given by his master.[68] In this case one was given a gift, an opportunity to change his/her life and failed to take advantage of that gift.

It is hard to fathom sometimes, but the bad things that happen to us are actually gifts. Bad things provide one with the opportunity to grow and improve, to be a better person. When one recognizes the opportunity as a gift and makes changes to better him/herself due to the things learned from the bad event, a tragedy is transformed into a life changing positive event. It is part of God's plan to make you into the person that He brought you on earth to be. If one learns something that changes one's outlook on life or radically changes one's approach to salvation, then you have something special.

---

[68] Matthew 25:24-30. At the end of the Parable of Talents, Jesus admonishes the servant who buried his money given. Jesus was pointing out that gifts given by God must be used and shared and not hidden.

3. **God is involved in our lives every day.** Whether we are aware or not, God is involved and in control or our daily lives. We enjoy free will to make decisions the way we see the world, but God, in His mystery, orchestrates not only our lives, but the world around us. He has the plan. What we do and the decisions we make influence not only our lives but the world around us. God provides opportunities and gentle (or in some cases not so gentle) reminders to keep us on path for what He has planned and planned for our salvation. When we cooperate with God's plan, good things happen. If not, our world starts to crumble.

    God answers prayers of ours. God also answers those involuntary prayers that give us those epiphany moments of brilliance. God knows what is best for us and gives us all the opportunities to make the right decisions to take advantage of God's plan for us. The great end of the story: God also has infinite mercy and patience and will continue to prod and provide opportunities for us to get back on His path to salvation as long as we live.

4. **Listen to God's calls.** Be ready to say "Yes" or you will miss out on something spectacular. Always believe that you are capable to do something great. On the other hand, be ready to do something simple and ordinary in a loving way as well. Part of God's plan includes each and every one of us. One does not have to be an important or high profile person for God to choose to make a change in our world through one of us. He may just pick some nobody from Indianapolis or Plano to cause a big ripple in this world, be it locally or beyond. He may pick you. Be ready to say "Yes" and be patient to wait for God's work to be done through you. The Lord's call may not be as spectacular as a fire. It may be such as Elisha's call where he heard God's voice in a subtle tiny breeze. You may be called to just talk to someone. Just a word or even a smile could change someone's life. Who knows, the one person that is really affected and changed by your good action may be you yourself. Also remember that your "Yes" may be the

beginning of a chain of invitations that God has ready to make available to others. A "No" answer thwarts and cuts off any chance of that good works chain to happen.

5. **God cares for all people**. He wants to draw all people near to Him. He created us and, as said in the creation story of Genesis, *"God looked at everything he had made, and found it very good"*[69]. From our fire story, one can see how God took care of my family and me. Also, through the story, one can see that God answers prayers of His people. He always provides, through His fatherly nurturing, by answering our prayers when and how we need. Sometimes the answers to our prayers and needs do not come in a way or timing that we expect, or is contrary to what we see as an appropriate answer to our situational needs. Remember, God is not a genie with a magic lamp to instantly grant your free wishes. Again, the Lord has an infinite time vantage point to see not only how a response to a prayer affects our life, but how it affects the world and the Lord's ultimate plan for humanity.

Sometimes it seems that God never answers our prayers, or it seems that the opposite from what was prayed for happens. Sometimes He allows local, national and global tragedies to wake His people up. Sometimes He allows bad things to happen to us individually, such as house fires, job losses, and bad financial situations. In the end, God always leads the world, through His will, for the betterment of us and humanity as a whole.

I heard a great minute sermon one Saturday Mass years ago about Jesus' Good Shepherd love. The priest described a friend traveling on a tour bus in the Israeli countryside. There were shepherds, tending their flocks on the hills, to the one side of the road, so the scene looked so Biblical to his friend. The friend sees a little lamb bolt from one of the shepherds'

---

[69] Genesis 1:31

flocks and the shepherd leaves the flock initiating his move to recover the sheep back to the flock. The friend made the bus driver stop so he could photograph the event. He envisioned the Good Shepherd scene of the shepherd lovingly carrying the lamb on his shoulders back to the flock. The friend was all set with his camera to record this Biblical reenactment. Well, as the shepherd reached the lamb, instead of picking the lamb up and carrying it back, he hauled off and gave the lamb a sharp kick in its hind quarters, sending it scampering back to the flock. The Priest's final comment was, *"That is just how God responds to us. Sometimes he lovingly picks us up, puts us on his shoulders and carries us back to the flock. Other times we get a kick in the rear. It depends on what God knows that we need."* For me, that kick in the pants, not only to me but my community as well, was burning my house down to energize the people surrounding me.

6. **Every person has Jesus in their hearts**. As I encountered after the fire, each person that came to our aid had Jesus within them. I know because I saw Him. Jesus is in all's hearts and He desperately wants each person to share Him with the rest of the world. By sharing one's Jesus, this allows more of Jesus' grace to enter one's heart – the Jesus already there plus the Jesus someone else shares back. Sometimes it takes a little boost to get Jesus to bust out, but He is there. This is why every person in the world, poor to rich, good to bad can and does make a difference in the world. Just think of what a better place this world would be if everyone recognized that they had Jesus in their hearts and actively shared Jesus with others they came into contact with.

Again, per the example of the Parable of the Talents, Jesus does not want us to hoard the Jesus that has been given and implanted into our hearts. When we share our imbedded Jesus with another, we do not lose any of the Jesus we had originally, but actually there is a mutual additional reception of grace, Jesus, within us. We both gain, not lose. You now become instead of the servant given one Talent, you now become the one given five, thus reaping an additional five. Now, just think of the ripple effect that happens from the workings of an intentional discipleship type community that is geared to share Jesus with everyone they meet. Just think of the ripple effect that develops, as the amount of Jesus and grace that builds first within the initial people interacting, then spreads outward to the world as one act of kindness and charity begets another. Every time a person shares Jesus with a fellow neighbor, both that person as well as the neighbor, gains additional shares of Jesus' love and presence within them. Now if that person shares Jesus with five others followed by those five sharing with an additional five, eventually that would be neighborhood, city, state, country and even world changing, world salvific.

This world changing movement would have been set in action, starting with one person's sharing their Jesus! You can change the world. Just start a Jesus sharing ripple revolution.

7. **Each person makes the world a better place**. Again, no matter how rich, poor, important, lowly, young or old, good or bad, a person is or behaves, each and every person makes the world a better place just because that person is in the world. Each person created was done so for a reason and a purpose by God. Even if the only thing the world learns from a person is what not to do to keep in God's graces, the world has learned a wonderful lesson and thus becomes a better place. This is why abortion and euthanasia are so devastating to the world.

Even in the case of the worst possible person – let us say, one like Hitler – who put the world into war and murdered millions of Jews, Catholics, people with birth defects, etc., even still one could argue that Hitler made the world a better place. Sometimes we need a really bad example of a human being to show us how bad and low the human mind is capable to work – when God is removed from one's life. Although we, as humans, cannot be the final judge of anyone's actions or whether one ends up in Heaven or Hell, the heinous behavior of such as Hitler's will be thusly judged by the Almighty, *"Their penalty is what they deserve."*[70]

Before Hitler, humans of this world could not fathom that a person could sink so low to perform and orchestrate such atrocities as he did through the Holocaust. We, the world, looked the other way in disbelief that, surely this could not have been true, and took no action. We now look at things such as genocide differently. Not that the world is absolutely intolerant of atrocities, because they still go on. We still look the other way – just look at what we in our own country have done since 1972 killing tens of millions unborn babies and legally under the protection of the law of the land. We do though have the knowledge, due to people such as Hitler, of the power and the seductiveness of evil and its ability to sway hearts to do and perform unthinkable dark things against humanity. We see the human mind's ability to justify things as acceptable that are totally heinous. The Holocaust has challenged us as a human race and empowered/challenged us to speak up in the face of evil and speak and listen to the truth; to come to the assistance of the people that are vulnerable and in need; to fight evil at all costs. Yes, sometimes the world even needs examples of what not to do to make it better.

On the other hand, what celebration happens when one who thrives living on the dark side repents and turns the corner to serve the Lord? The Bible has many references to the infinite mercy that God has. *"Upon his arrival home, he calls together his friends and neighbors and says to them, 'Rejoice with me because I have found my lost sheep.' I tell you, in just the same way there will be more joy in heaven over one sinner who repents than over ninety-nine righteous people who have no need of repentance."*[71]

---

[70] Romans 3:8
[71] Luke 15:6-7

God also makes His forgiveness available right up to the point of death. Bible stories such as the workers employed to work in the vineyard where all workers, even those hired at the very end of the day, were given the entire daily wage[72]. Then there is the story of the Good Thief at the scene of the Crucifixion. It demonstrates that a person living contrary to God's law can obtain Salvation even at the very end of life[73]. So, at the end of one's life, no matter what one has done in one's life – even Hitler I dare say – we are there on our own cross planted there with Jesus. The ultimate question is now posed, "Which one are you, the one on the left or the one on the right; the one that accepts or rejects Jesus and His forgiveness?" I am very confident that a great many great sinners are now with Jesus in heaven because of their final deathbed repentance. Now that is not only a good but a glorious day!

Eliminating people though, whether be via abortion, euthanasia or some other method of ethnic or religious cleansing, is devastating to our families, communities, country and world. The thought that killing the unborn will somehow reduce crime, poverty, or somehow make this world a better place is a total sham, an awful lie. Anytime we as humans play God and try to help God along to make things "better" for humanity, it always ends in disaster. It is as though some people think they know how to solve the world's problems better than God does! Those responsible for this and other atrocities against God will be thusly and justly asked to account for their actions upon meeting their Maker at the end of life. As stated above, everyone, even the persons living contrary to Jesus' teachings will have their day on the cross to either repent and be welcomed to Heaven, or not and be judged accordingly.

---

[72] Matthew 20:1-16
[73] Luke 23:32-43 The Crucifixion narrative.

There used to be a margarine commercial years ago that had a slogan that said, *"It's not nice to fool Mother Nature."*[74] The same can be said about people that think they can do a better job controlling population than God does. *"'An enemy has done this.' His slaves said to him, 'Do you want us to go and pull them up? He replied, 'No, if you pull up the weeds you might uproot the wheat along with them."*[75] Any time an innocent person is removed from this earth through a man conceived and induced method, it makes the world less Godlike. It foils the role that God had in mind for that person. In the end, the world loses. As the Bible verse here says, trying to remove the bad using human methods of extermination not only eliminates a lot of good wheat, but the whole field is worse off in the end. We lose the contribution – good or bad – that the person would have made to make this world a better place.

8. **God rewards people who do His will**. God gave my family far more rewards vs. what we lost because we said "Yes" to be a part of His plan. From the Spiritual to financial, my family and I were in a much better condition after than before. Do not be afraid to say "Yes" to God's callings. God's plan may take you way out of your comfort zone or deal you with what looks like a crushing loss, but in the end God knows what He is doing in His infinite wisdom. God loves us dearly and infinitely. Per Mother Teresa's earlier quote, *"I know God won't give me anything I can't handle"*. Not that God won't challenge the boundaries, but in the end, it is totally worth the effort or suffering that God has gifted you with. If one goes through the effort in a loving way to do His will, Jesus rewards us 100 fold. This is why, when Jesus calls His men to the Priesthood, if one has the courage to heed God's call, the rewards are a lifetime of wonder and grace. People that miss their Vocational callings miss a grand opportunity to be in line

---

[74] Chiffon margarine TV advertisement that began running from 1971 and through the 80's to advertise their margarine tasted just like butter.
[75] Matthew 13:28-29

with God's plan. Sometimes that call is hard to understand or to wrap one's head around. That is where Faith and prayer takes hold, that saying "Yes" will result in immense blessings and graces.

9. **Everyone is part of God's plan.** Things that you do or happen to you may not be obvious at the time why they happened, who they benefited, or see that any good at all was done. The result may be invisible to you and many. What happened to you may actually be an accumulative effect from one or many other exposures to God's will that happened to other people at other occasions. Each happened separately through other people combining to produce a grand result in God's overall plan. The full effect may be months, years or even centuries away from developing. Again, the real recipient(s) of the effects of my fire story may not even be born yet. However insignificant your good or bad event looks to you in the grand scheme of things, have Faith that it is somehow part of God's grand plan.

Do not discount the little things that you do or are called to do and how they fit into God's plan. Even though one perceives his/her act as insignificant in one's own eyes, the deed is in itself very significant in God's eyes. We see and rank things with human eyes. The smile or hand shake may play a big role in the salvation of that receiving person. That insignificant smile or hand shake may even start a chain reaction that saves many more in the future.

Refrain from the need for "immediate reaction/gratification"; the feeling that if I do something good for a person, I should expect an immediate positive response; a glorious "Thank you, you saved my life" moment. Remember, we are seed planters. Sometimes it takes the seed a while to germinate. Do not despair if you are not around to see the fruits of your deed done. *"For here the saying is verified that 'One sows and another reaps.'*"[76] For instance, if you give a good book to an individual to read, do you expect that person to sit right down and start reading and enjoying the book? What if the person files the book away? Does the book not do good five years from then when the person becomes intrigued enough to read the book? What if the person you gave the book to was not actually the one that God really intended to read it? What If God really meant this book to be read by this person's brother who happened to come along and find it at his brother's house? Remember, we operate in God's will and God's time. Things will happen when and to whom their time is right. We just need to say "Yes" to Jesus' bidding and plant the seed. Have peace, it is enough to plant the seed even if someone else gets to watch the seed grow.

10. **Life is Biblical.** It was amazing especially when writing this book how easy it was to find Biblical references that went paralleled to what was happening and what I was feeling. That is because people written in the Bible are just like us today. People that wrote the books of the Bible are just like us.

I look at my life so far and to date and saw my life laid out within the Old Testament passages. I saw when I was close to God, I was strong. I could do or overcome any hardship that I may have found myself in and had great joy. I also saw when I wandered away from God, I was weak. Things started to go wrong and nothing seemed to make sense any more. I definitely felt lost, alone and seemed that I was unable to control things that were happening to me in my life at that time. In those times of darkness, I could not really put my finger on what was missing. Next, I could see the joy that I had when returning back to God, reminiscent of the Prodigal

---

[76] John 4:37

Son[77], where Jesus met me with open arms and said, "Welcome home my son".

Biblical icons such as the Old Testament Hebrews and New Testament Pharisees did good things; they did bad things. They had great belief; they lost their belief. Good things happened to them; bad things happened to them. Regardless, God called and spoke to them every day. God loved them every day. God challenged them every day to come into a closer and more loving relationship with Him. Sometimes God allowed them His wake up calls. The same thing happens today to each of us and to the world around us.

I found after comparing life in the Biblical periods of time vs. ours today, although happened in a much earlier age with different types of possessions, transportation and entertainment etc., the Old Testament was a microcosm of the life that goes on today. The Old Testament Bible did a great job to chronicling life as it was in the generations before Christ, including the documentation of human concupiscence. Biblical authors showed us the good as well as the warts. We can look at the Old Testament and be exalted and mentored by their extreme Faith in God; the Faith to go into battle and be certain that God was fighting on their side in spite of what looked on paper as insurmountable odds against. We also saw examples of poor behavior and loss/lack of faith that we need to avoid to gain Salvation. The Bible identified bad behaviors

---

[77] Luke 15:11-32 Youngest son takes his total inheritance from his father, travels off and squanders his fortune to then live destitute after his inheritance runs out. He then returns home planning to live like a slave because he squandered his father's inheritance on vice and personal pleasures; that he no longer deserved to be treated as his father's son. His father sees him in the distance coming home and runs to greet him with unconditional love and joy to welcome the son back to the family. This shows God's infinite mercy and the joy given by the return back of a soul previously lost.

and emphasized their punishments by God; the consequences of those actions. The Bible, best of all, chronicled God's eternal love and mercy by continuously forgiving and reinstating His graces back to his Chosen People in spite of the many gross and even heinous transgressions committed, even by some of the most beloved and most vaulted heroes, e.g. David's repentance after the murder of Uriah in order to marry his wife Bathsheba.[78]

We can look toward the Bible to set our own lives' path to Salvation. We can look to the Old Testament to gain incentive to lead a clean life and constantly search for God in everything we do. We can take solace that we will have ups and downs in our spiritual lives, such as the Hebrews did, and that God is there for us to come back to when we are ready to repent and move on.

We can look to the New Testament for additional challenges. It challenges us not to be minimalists, looking for what is the least I can do to be saved, but to always ask and pursue how I can be and how I can get closer to God; to follow Jesus' examples and teachings more fully. One can also be uplifted by the Faith and zeal demonstrated by the Apostles and early Christians who many lost everything including their lives to gain everything – their Eternal Reward. If those broken but outwardly passionate Christian humans can do what they did for Christ, who are we to say that we are not capable of the same zeal and love of Jesus? Be part of the prayer!

---

[78] 2Samuel chapters 11, 12 After the profit Nathan confronted David that God was aware of his grave sins of lust, adultery and murder due to his encounter with Bathsheba and the murder of her husband, Uriah, he realized that he greatly sinned against God and repented. God then forgave David after he repented. As a punishment though, God did take David's first son born to him and Bathsheba. God then allowed David and his next son by Bathsheba, Solomon, to continue the greatness of Israel, which was the high point in Hebrew history.

11. **Charity is explosive.** When charity develops wonderful things can happen. It's amazing, when one allows Jesus to work through and to come out of them in love, mercy and charity, great joy ensues. Following Jesus' challenge to *"love your neighbor as yourself"*[79] is a difficult command. There are always reservations one has to really make oneself vulnerable; to give of one's self to another, especially to a stranger or even an enemy; to give one's unconditional love and charity. I am fully in tuned to this feeling because I am guilty as charged here as well.

    The key requirement to love one's neighbor is to truly love yourself first. If one does not love him/herself first, how can one understand how to love one's neighbor as one's self? To love yourself, one first needs to understand and come to grips that you are a son/daughter of God and that God infinitely loves and cares for you.

    The sad thing is, despite how good one feels after performing an act of true charity, it is amazing how our human brain works. Since charity feels so good after it is done, why would we not want to live our lives in constant and total charity? Our human nature though, combats that good feeling because we cannot stand to be out there vulnerable for long periods of times. That is why people like Mother Teresa are or are about to become Saints, because in their lives, they were able to fight their instincts to reduce the risk of getting hurt, to stay engaged in unconditional love and charity. We are truly blessed that God has given us these wonderful Saint role models to show us that every one of us is capable of Sainthood if we fight our worldly instincts and focus on doing God's will.

12. **Be a Beatitudinal person.** I realize Beatitudinal is not a real word, but let's go ahead and give Webster a new one to define.

---

[79] Matthew 22:39

What is being Beatitudinal? To be Beatitudinal, one must be courageous to heed God's callings. To be Beatitudinal, one must have the courage and the Faith to live in this world but not be a part of this world. It means taking a radical view of Jesus' message. At the Sermon on the Mount, Jesus did not tell the crowd, "I know you are all good people so here are some good words to live by." No, the message Jesus conveyed to them was one of radical change; He was making known what it took to really know and follow Him. These were totally counter cultural and counter intuitive commands He gave them and as well to us. It identified the level of Christianity that He challenges us to be, who can unconditionally and freely shed his/her membership and allures of this world, endure harsh persecution and follow in Jesus' sandals; to take up Jesus' cross.

A Beatitudinal person is not a wimp. A Beatitudinal person is not some soft wall flower that doesn't want to rock the boat; to do something that might make someone uncomfortable or angry at them. A Beatitudinal person is not afraid to be a peacemaker; to stand up for and obey Christ's Church and Its teachings; to stand up for your neighbor when he/she/they are being persecuted, even at the risk of being drawn into their persecution. To risk your treasure to give to the poor. The courage it takes to turn one's cheek when attacked.

One cannot look to and live by the Beatitudes as a fluffy confirmation that your life is good because you are kind of represented by all those eight Blesseds mentioned. Live the Beatitudes as the radical challenge toward salvation that Jesus meant them to be. If you ask God to make you a Beatitudinal person, be prepared for some radical changes that will rock your world – in a good way of course. Go ahead and ask!

13. **Be prepared for what you ask God for – He may just give it to you.** I will start off by saying, there is no better or joyous feeling than there is when one does the work of the Lord. That being said, I would say that commitment of one's life, to give

God carte blanche with your life, can be a scary thing to contemplate because you never know just how much carte blanche the Lord will take once given the opening to do so.

Have peace though. As mentioned by Mother Teresa, God does not give you more than you are capable to handle. A good prayer regimen is recommended along with your wish to allow God in to do what He wills for you. This way you have a good dialogue going with our Lord as the cards start to fall in place. I recommend asking Jesus often what He has called or planned for you.

Here is a good recent example of how God sometimes works when you give Him the OK to use you as He wills. In March of this year, things were going smoothly for Cathy and me. Both were working, and our savings account was actually growing rather than shrinking. On Thursday March 12, I said a prayer to God to use me as he needed. Things happened fast. Saturday, I received an email from our HR VP that I was supposed to come to a meeting that Monday (3-16). When I arrived for the meeting, I found that I had been laid off. Lord, I did not see that one coming. I instantly said a prayer and said, "OK, now you have my attention again. What do You want me to do for You?" Well, I think this book is what he had in mind – I hope.

Not every time when you give the Lord your life does he do something to "really get your attention". There have been other times in my life, after I discussed with the Lord to use me as He needed, where the Lord did not resort to any obvious outgoing measures, but quite possibly He did use me in subtler ways. But as you can see by my two occasions, one needs to be ready to accept whatever the Lord's will is when you give Him your life to use. You might just get something a little more radical than you thought you asked for. I say that tongue in cheek because whatever the Lord gives you will end up to be so fantastic in the end that words will not be able to express – so ask away and pray a lot!

14. **Feel free to put yourself out of your comfort zone and share your time, talent and treasure.** Pope Benedict XVI once said, *"Do not be afraid of Christ! He takes away nothing and He gives you everything. When we give ourselves to him, we receive a hundredfold in return. Yes, open, open wide the doors to Christ – and you will find true life."* When hearing such a quote or statement from a Pope, I always tend to say, "That is easy for you to say because you are a Pope." God calls us daily to be Him for someone or groups. It is up to us, with our free will, to take the first step. Will we say "Yes" or "No" to God's call? If we say "No" we gain nothing. At best we keep status quo. We act lukewarm. When we step from our comfort zone and step out with the Lord, great things start happening. First, one feels freer than before because one's comfort zone, holding him/her back, was conquered and now has grown larger. One less shackle now holds you back from God's true grace and love. Second, comes the feeling of joy and accomplishment that the Lord called, you listened, and obeyed. You may not have been able to see signs of the fruits of your effort. You may only see the seed planted. Just completing a call from Jesus itself, puts one in a joyous state. The call might be to just turn around and talk to the person you do not know behind you in church, or a kind word to a person passing by. Go ahead and take that step, that leap of Faith, to hear and follow God's calls in your daily life. You might just change someone's life – or yours as well.

15. **Prayer is powerful.** We can do amazing things through prayer. I used to think that prayer was just something to do to tide over until the thing I was praying for either came together or did not. I always heard in parochial school that God answers all my prayers. I really had a hard time wrapping my head around that statement, because it seemed quite random. Sometime the prayer was answered and sometimes it seemed

# I Have Come To Set The Earth On Fire

that it was not. I did not get that fancy air rifle for Christmas that I prayed for.

It was not until my CRHP and fire experience that I truly felt the magnificent power of prayer. First, just the power of being able to talk to and be in a personal relationship with Jesus was so wonderful and peaceful. When the fire happened and fulfilled what Jesus conveyed to me, that was so over the top wonderful and astonishing. I was totally flabbergasted that I would be part of a plan put together by my God and that I was standing at ground zero watching it happen right in front of my eyes. I look back fondly on those days and wish that I could have that closeness again with our Lord that I had then.

Then, for the first time, I can truly point to my and other's prayers as being answered when my two CRHP friends' children were cured of cancer! The feeling of being heard by the Almighty Lord; the feeling that of all the billions of people out there in the world, he chose to hear the prayers of these lowly, humble servants asking for His intercession. He looked at our individual petitions and granted our prayer. In the Book of Matthew, Jesus commented that Faith the size of a mustard seed could move mountains[80]. If it is within God's will, faith the size of mine – less than a mustard seed – added with others, can cure cancer. I just remember being so joyous hearing that God's mercy and grace was bestowed on those two children of my friends that I could almost burst. The one thing I had to keep reminding myself was, my part in these two mini miracles had nothing directly to do about me being one of the ones praying. I personally did not save these two. It was God working in conjunction with and interceding with my and others' prayers that cured these people. It was all God. But it did show that He definitely <u>knew who I was</u> and that He <u>loved me</u> enough to grant my prayer. If God knows me

---

[80] Matthew 17:20

personally, that also means that God knows YOU personally as well! Wow! That is a life changing thought!

# I Have Come To Set The Earth On Fire

# Chapter 19: Final Concluding Thoughts

The final chapter has to start and end with the Apostle John's total and encompassing description of God. Three short words, nine letters that sum this whole book up as well as His Church and the Bible itself.

> *"God Is Love"*[81]

> *"For God so loved the world that he gave his only Son, so that everyone who believes in him might not perish but might have eternal life."*[82]

Not only did God so love the world that He sent His Only Son, but He loves you and me so infinitely, so passionately that He is willing, like the father that He is, to push, encourage, prod, pull, and slyly hint unceasingly to get us, even in spite of our human free will, to say "Yes" to Him. To lead us to our Heavenly rewards. To share our infinite Heavenly bliss with Him for ever and ever.

Now, to some of the bystanders of my life's ups and downs, it may not have seemed to them that a house burning down or a job lost could be such a great, wonderful and spiritual experience. To the wrong mind set, these could be seen as failures and catastrophes; events where one sees everything that was lost and nothing of what was gained. Well, the same was said of Jesus dying on the cross. The mode of death for a loser, the criminal, the outcast, the hated person – at least by the powers to be. It was seen as the evidence of the failure of another fake messiah by the Jewish factions that were against Jesus. In the end the cross still stands as the emblem of the highest accomplishment, the highest display of love, the biggest win in human history. The cross that was then followed by the Resurrection. The cross that propelled the salvation of now countless people in Heaven. The cross that toppled mammoth regimes from the powerful Romans to the Communists in 1989 without firing a shot.

---

[81] 1 John 4:8
[82] John 3:16

The people who have failed to see what was gained by my family's situations have missed the point; the point of learning that God had put right in their lap for the taking. Again, hopefully someday at least one or more of these doubting persons will "get it". It may be a time that one's memory thinks back under different circumstances. The fire experience may have been an early seed planted that another occurrence(s) finishes the story. I hope and pray that this is the case. Whatever mode this story can play in someone's salvation story, the story will have accomplished its goal if only one takes these experiences to gain a closer relationship with Jesus, our Lord.

I learned that sometimes God asks me to just be there to do His will. God's will does not always require some heroic action, courageously riding into battle. In the fire event, all God asked me to do was to get out of my burning home with my family, then stand back and watch God take over from there. If I let pride enter into my heart and refused the help from my fellow brothers, I would have messed the whole thing up.

One needs to pray to really discern what God is asking one to do. God may be asking you for a heroic effort to make a grand stand. Maybe God is really asking you to be a prayer warrior to pray for the real person God has in mind to hear His calling and come forth. In the end one needs to step away from what "I" want or think should be done and let God run the show.

**It Is Finished**

Ending this story has been a tough thing to complete. As I have been reliving my experiences and thinking back at what they meant and what The Holy Spirit was wanting me to put down for all to read, it has definitely served to rekindle some of the Spiritual feelings and emotions that I felt during those months before and after the fire. Perhaps all God wanted me to write as the summary for this book is what was said on the beginning line of the Conclusion chapter, *"God is love"*. Does that not say it all?

So now I commence my work to conclude the fire story. My story and my reason for my hope. The beginning of Luke and the end of John's Gospels accurately assess my overall feelings when writing this book. First Luke, *"I too have decided, after investigating everything accurately anew, to write it down in an orderly sequence for you"*[83]. Then there is John, *"There are also many other things that Jesus did, but if these were to be described individually, I do not think the whole world would contain the books that would be written."*[84] I feel that there were so many wondrous things that Jesus did and revealed to me during the fire episode that there are just not sufficient human words in the dictionary and enough of them to really do justice to all what Jesus did for and through us.

As the fire story has been recapped by the pages before, it documents how complex yet how glorious the workings of God are. Yet it also shows the simplicity of God's love. All we have to do is listen to Him, say "Yes", and then watch as the magnificence of God's will happen through Jesus and the Holy Spirit. It demonstrates the length Jesus goes to save His lambs, to bring His lambs back to the fold. The fact that He first selected me, selected my family to enter into His prayer, His plan; to select us to be the instruments that His salvific grace was metered out to all the participants involved, is just mind boggling! Why us? I cannot answer that question. Possibly we were chosen because God knew we would say "Yes"; be willing participants to the asking's of His will.

What God asked my family to endure and accomplish was a totally radical experience for us. Even more radical than the loss of all our possessions was the wonderful and glorious response from our communities and the other gifts of love that we received from God. Just the thought of what was required of my family that early morning of July 5, 1996 is still a scary thing to contemplate. The price of that event almost had disastrous ramifications for my family and me. "Almost" is the correct term though, for again the Lord does not give us more than we can handle.

---

[83] Luke 1:3
[84] John 21:25

The event did take me especially way out of my original comfort zone. I think that was the most frightening aspect for me looking back. I endured and accomplished things far eclipsing what my "personal comfort box" allowed. With this experience, the thought that God could call me again to another radical change to my comfort zone still makes me feel uneasy. With my experiences documented, I know that I have, so far, been able to accept and persevere any test that God has laid in front of me. The one thing that I am sure of, if he asks me to relinquish all my possessions again or become unemployed per His will, I know I am capable and willing to do so. I am also sure that God is not done with us yet.

Day in and day out before and after the fire, God indeed asked and prodded me to leave my comfort zone and do his bidding. Sometimes I said "Yes", others I failed and said "No", or "Not now Lord, I am not ready yet." Some of these callings were the minor steps outside my comfort box, such as a smile that I should have given to a passerby stranger. Other larger leaps were asked for, but I decided to do it my way instead. The important thing is to become better equipped to recognize a situation that God places in front of you to do His will. How many times have we all misread a golden opportunity put in front of us by God, to do His will, and missed it? Afterwards, the ramifications of this opportunity missed was grasped. Next comes the fleeting feeling that if we could do it all over again and had another chance at that same opportunity, we would have acted differently to accomplish what Jesus had in mind for us. Good thing that God gives us plenty of chances to do his will. Jumping outside of my comfort box usually first starts with a scary leap of Faith, but through the fire story I now have a different perspective to respond to God's calls.

An uninformed bystander may fail see that all the fuss and adversity my family went through as worth the effort given. One, looking only at the immediate plane of play, would not have the forethought to recognize the beginnings of God's work and God's plan in action. That person would probably see a tragedy unfolding rather than God's plan in action. That person may not fathom that Newton's third law of physics actually fits in quite well here to describe what happened – every action produces an opposite reaction. The fire – bad action – produced a glorious reaction –energizing of the spirituality of the people we came into contact with, or who came into contact with our story that fateful day.

Where God's rendition of the third law of physics differs a bit from Newton's version, first, that reaction does not necessarily have to happen and be realized right away. It may take minutes, hours, years or even centuries to bear its intended fruit. Secondly, the reaction in God's realm does not have to be "equal" as the third law states. In the fire's case, the glorious reaction far exceeded the fire loss action by a very large margin. God makes his own laws; in fact, He makes all the laws – including Newton's third law of physics.

Hopefully through the readership of this book, the effect of God's grace and love on you will continue to grow. Hopefully the reaction of reading the contents of this book has brought the reader closer to our Lord Almighty. As stated earlier, possibly the real person or persons that the fire experience is meant to touch may not even have been born yet. Maybe the person meant to be touched is you. I must have faith that any loving good work done in God's name will indeed have a profound benefit as per God's plan. Again, performing good works is not a chore done to gain or purchase salvation. It is a duty mandated by Jesus' teachings to love one's neighbors. To love one's neighbor means to do what one can possibly do to aid my neighbor to attain his/her Salvation and reach his/her Heavenly Reward.

Another thing that I hope my readers see in my Faith journey is, the fire episode was not a cure all event that served to provide me with everlasting unbridled Faith in God. I still struggle. I struggle to hear God's call. I still struggle to die to self and say "Yes" to the greatest, most infinite lover and my most infinite benefactor. One can see how the recovery of my worldly goods since the fire has renewed my distractions which inhibits me from clearly hearing Jesus' intimate voice; to hear and feel the Holy Spirit's fire that should be totally enveloping my life. I still struggle to give my unconditional love and trust to God. I am guilty of first looking at and fearing what I may lose by saying "Yes" to God, by allowing God to take total control of my life to do what He wills. I still have the tendency to "look both ways before crossing the street" before answering Gods callings.

With all that I went through during the fire, it would seem that I would have a stronger "if I can survive that, I can take whatever God throws my way" mind set. I should be able to unconditionally do whatever God asks me to do. I still; however, have that anchor holding me back; that box of comfort that I still have trouble getting out of. My possessions and my ego still carry too much value and pulls me toward that line away from Jesus' outstretched hands.

The sad thing is that I have seen God's glory happen. I have felt His deep love for my family and me. Yet I still choose to forgo this Heaven on earth in order to cater to me, to my failings, my shortcomings; living on my own terms instead of His. I struggle because I have seen and felt God's glory and would love to get back to that place. The spirit is willing but the body is struggling with the "me" part to get back there.

The challenge now to the readers of this book is to find your fire story and not let go. The challenge is to incorporate the learnings and keep growing closer to God from that point on. Everyone's Faith journey is just that – a journey royal. It starts right here where you are at right now, and you either grow closer to God or farther away. Each day, each minute, one has the opportunity to embrace Jesus' teachings and let Him draw you closer and closer to Him. Never give up. Never give in. Never be satisfied with where your relationship is with our Lord until the day you depart from this earth. That is the path to Salvation.

The fire experience also gives me a good pause for joy and encouragement about the character of our fellow citizens of this world. The amount of goodness I witnessed from our communities was utterly astonishing. The level of response we received was totally out of this world – into the Godly spectrum one might say.

The face of humanity that is typically shown to us in TV shows, movies or one finds in newspaper or on CNN news stories, usually portrays the human essence as one of defiance of God and the frustration of one's fight for "my" share of what "I" deserve and did not get. The CNN version of life is totally contrary to God's reality and the reality that I experienced during the fire story. God's reality may not make for good 24-7 news reporting, but there is real Christian fire out there and billions of good people that are all traveling on their Faith journeys searching for peace, love and salvation. St. Augustine said in his book *"Confessions"* that one's heart is restless and continues to search until it finds rest in the Lord.

I found that through events – good or tragic, such as our fire story – they bring out the good in the human heart and make it visible for all to see. I was most fortunate to have had the opportunity to witness the face of unconditional love and mercy that gushed out from my fellow brothers and sisters coming to our aid.

The first indication about the depth of the goodness written in my fellow man's heart was the sheer number of people that came to our aid after the fire. I did not expect to see more than a few family members and close friends pitch in. In reality, hundreds of people played a prominent role in the charity given, assisting my family back on our feet. Acts of generosity and kindness were provided by a wide range of people from all walks of life; from those we had come into close contact with as well as a large number that we possibly only came into remote proximity contact with at best. This outburst of love by our community really defines, as Jesus did, who are my brothers. As Jesus said, any pagan can love the people that love them back. The real Christian, as these people were, gave unconditional love even to people that they did not really know. A majority of the people, who came to our aid, gave even though we probably may never meet again, let alone reciprocate their kindness. Reciprocation was not a condition to their charity.

Secondly, the immediacy of the response – there was no hesitation from our local communities. There was no delay in people's' resolve that we needed help, they had the help to give, and gave it. Charity burst out even before the embers had a chance to cool. The range of things given and offered to us to get us back on our feet, kept us totally fed, clothed and housed until our insurance funds were received. We were not want for anything. Immediately the cooperative spirits of the people, touched by our situation, recognized our immediate needs for food, shelter, and clothing and provided without hesitation. The gifts of money, other items and other random acts of kindness given to help us push forward and get our lives back on track, was totally beyond anything I could fathom. All were given freely and with loving hearts. The glow of Jesus in their hearts was so bright, knowing they had been called to participate in something special and had said their "Yes" to do their part in God's will and plan. They became part of God's prayer. I have never seen anything so beautiful as the glow seen in each person's face as they completed their act of charity.

The people in the Lawrence and Castleton townships of Indianapolis, IN gave a wonderful accounting of themselves. The rush of kindness and charity received shows that the people here in the US are truly blessed and capable of wonderful and powerful things to celebrate and promote the Kingdom of God here on earth. The reaction given showed that we are all capable of doing God's will. We have, etched into each one of our hearts, that capability and the burn to do charitable things and be Jesus to our fellow brothers on earth. Life gets so easy, so simple and beautiful when we are able to discover Jesus in our hearts and then sit back and let Jesus take over.

So, the book comes down to this one question: Who are my brothers, my family and my friends?[85] How does one define "brothers, family, and friends"? It comes down to one thing: Love! We discovered that we cannot survive in this world without our brothers, family and friends. As shown by the early Christians, we share this world, the good and the bad, together with all humanity. Without brothers, family and friends there is no way for us to get to Heaven by ourselves. We need our brothers, family and friends to be our mentors, our protectors, our benefactors. We individually also need our brothers, family and friends to be a conduit to share our God given gifts; to fulfill our mandated duty to follow Jesus' commandments to

---

[85] Matthew 12:48

help those in need; to do our best to bring as many people with us to our Eternal Salvation.

We found that, by the sheer numbers of friends that we had that came forward over the weeks after the fire, we were truly blessed. A situation such as the fire really gives a vision as to how many true friends one has. To have that many people that would come forward, have my back, and give of their own time, talent and treasure to assist a fellow brother in need, just makes me feel like I am the wealthiest man alive. I never knew I had so many people in my life that had such affection for my family and me. The vision of the wealth of friendship was another big gift that I received from God for my family's troubles and for saying "Yes" to do and allow His will to be done.

The essentialness of the family unit became another crucial topic to come from the fire story. The true gift of the family that God has not only given to me, but He has also given the family unit to the whole of human race as well. I could not have survived the fire without the love and support of my family. They were there for me. I was there for them. They gave me their love and support. I gave them my love and support. That is how a family works! With the love and support of my family I never felt threatened. I never felt in danger. I never felt that the burden of losing home and all possessions was more than we could handle. We got through this as a family and it made us even stronger. The old saying that what doesn't kill you makes you stronger was an understatement here. What I received and what I saw from my family during the fire experience was Jesus' agape love. Going through this traumatic experience with my family gave me some insights to the strength, perseverance and overall family bond the Holy Family must have exhibited through all the turmoil and danger that they had to live through when Jesus was an infant and growing up – because they were a family christened and blessed by God. A family sticks together through thick and thin. You know, I never thought of the wedding vow that Cathy and I took together 36 years ago also applies to the family as well. As a family we take each other for sickness and health, good times and bad until death do we part.

I hope this story has given you a little feel of what it is like to actually be called by God to do His will. In my experience, the act God asked was a radical event in my family's life. As stated early in the book, the fire story has become the demarcation marker of time in my family's existence. My experience shows that the event was radical, demanding and even dangerous, but for all the worldly things lost, God provided much more. God even trained me, got me ready, and made me spiritually strong enough to withstand the tough challenge that was ahead. In the manner that God prepared me, the challenge was never more than I or my family could handle. In the end, doing God's will was the best thing that ever happened to me. If I had botched this up and not complied with God's will or stubbornly tried to go it alone, just look at all the wonders I would have missed. None of my fellow brothers and sisters we encountered would have been energized by the Holy Spirit and who knows what would have transpired, how lives could have possibly trended differently instead of upwards if Jesus' and the Holy Spirit's' love was thwarted. The world would have lost an opportunity to thrive in the glow of God's love and mercy. Peoples' good works bank accounts would not be as full.

My family had a chance and did become part of an enormous prayer to God. One that was so beautiful. A prayer that put the "Ave Maria" to shame. That early morning of the fire, I had a similar sensation compared to what the shepherds must have experienced in the field that night when Jesus was born where angels, hovering above them, sang *"Glory to God in the highest"*.[86] Becoming part of God's prayer gives peace and joy. A feeling that I have never had before or after the fire. Glory to God in the highest!

So, what is God calling you to do? Are you ready to step out from your comfort zone and say "Yes" to God's plan when called? What is your Faith temperature? Are you ready to increase your Faith temperature to the hot side past lukewarm? It is time to take a deep breath and start praying to God right now to make your mind and heart

---

[86] Luke 2:14

available to God's plan that He has in store for you. Let us do this together:

> *"Jesus, You know that I love You with all my heart, mind, body and soul. I am Yours. Everything that I have has been a gift from You. I deserve nothing, yet You have so loved me to give me all that I have. Lead me wherever and whatever You need me to do, go, or to be, for I will follow. Let me be an instrument of Your love. May I gladly and freely do Your bidding. I pray this in the name of Jesus our Lord. Amen"*

God's love can endure if we let ourselves become part of His prayer. God's Love needs to start with each one of us. As more of the world commits to enter into God's prayer, the world will be saved.

Thus, ends the love story between God, my family and the rest of the world. Well, I misspoke. The story never ends. Because…..

# *God is Love*
# *For Ever and Ever Amen!!!*

# I Have Come To Set The Earth On Fire

For more information about the author and book or to contact John:

        Website: www.hofpublications.org

        Email: hofpublications@gmail.com

Also, visit John's website to keep current with new inspirational and spiritually engaging posts.

After you finish reading "I Have Come to Set the Earth on Fire", please tell me what you think of my book. Also, I encourage you to go on line to your favorite book purchase website and post a review for the book.

God Bless and remember to always say "Yes" to God's will in your life. May the Lord's peace be with you always!

www.ingramcontent.com/pod-product-compliance
Lightning Source LLC
Chambersburg PA
CBHW071916290426
44110CB00013B/1377